NONPROFIT EXCELLENCE: STRATEGIES FOR A CHALLENGING WORLD

A HANDBOOK FOR GRANTMAKING AND NONPROFIT LEADERSHIP SKILLS

by

Louis J. Beccaria, Ph.D. and Constance Carter, CFRE

Cover design by Marie Moss, Artist, Philadelphia, PA

ISBN: 978-1-7367037-0-0

Printed in the United States of America

DEDICATION

We dedicate this book to those people

who devote their professional lives

every day to pursue mission-driven careers;

to those who philanthropically give their

financial resources; and to those who

volunteer their valuable time and expertise

in the spirit of making the world a better

place to live, work, and raise a family.

*As the cover illustrates, this book offers grantmakers and
nonprofit leaders a pathway out of the forest
of confusing and stressful situations
that frequently arise in our organizations.*

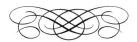

TABLE OF CONTENTS

Grantmaking-Related Documents

FOREWORD

Patricia (Tish) Mogan, M.A., M.B.A.
Standards for Excellence Director,
Pennsylvania Association of Nonprofit Organizations

Education is a lifelong process and opens us to new worlds and better ways to respond to people and situations. Education creates a more positive quality of life for individuals and for those with whom they interact.

This is exactly what this book offers to those who work in the nonprofit world. Board members and key staff will either confirm or strengthen what they already know and how they conduct themselves. They also will learn new ways to be more efficient and engaged to better support the mission and outcomes of a nonprofit.

Lou and Connie have extensive experience in working with the nonprofit sector. They have experienced what works and what does not work. They have learned important concepts and desire to pass these along. These concepts will enhance how the board operates as well as facilitate a trusted and productive relationship with the board and key staff.

Nonprofit Excellence: Strategies for a Challenging World can provide a means of continued education for board and staff. Pick an essay, share it with the board and staff, and then take some time to discuss this at a board meeting or other appropriate session. You can create your own set of questions for the discussion based on the current needs of your organization. *Nonprofit Excellence: Strategies for a Challenging World* provides a wide array of topics to consider. All are aimed at on-going education and adopting better and more productive ways of conducting board management for both seasoned and new board members.

Thanks to Connie and Lou for having the passion and will to put their experience in writing.

Happy reading and happy learning!

INTRODUCTION

Today, more than ever before, nonprofit organizations are often doing lifesaving, essential work throughout the world. Nonprofits frequently fill the gaps left by government programs that don't provide enough food, healthcare, education, and basic sustenance to keep people healthy and productive. They also venture into arenas government programs can't or won't often support, reaching far beyond them to care for animals, the environment, our history, the arts, religion, and more.

Paradoxically, nonprofit governance is left in the hands of volunteers who usually care deeply about their organizations' missions, but may have little or no training or guidance to go along with this commitment. All too often membership on a board is still dictated by who knows who or who can write the largest check, rather than on that person's skills or expertise. Compounding this situation is the fact that the Executive Director, generally a trained professional experienced in management and governance, is dependent on the volunteer board for their job.

Government agencies and some funders have increased their scrutiny of nonprofits in recent years, often in response to egregious instances of mismanagement, fraud, nepotism, and/or corruption. Yet for the average nonprofit that scrutiny is fairly superficial and comes with limited, if any, consequences.

The bottom line is that people who are serving in the nonprofit sector as volunteer board members, staff, or volunteers doing other types of work, need to police themselves, out of a deep commitment and passion to provide superior governance and support for our nonprofits.
No one else is going to do it – so we have to do it for ourselves.

The essays in this book focus on some of the most common and not so common governance and management challenges facing nonprofits today. Some of them may be totally new to you – others you may have worried about after a particularly disturbing conversation or board meeting. Each essay contains recommendations regarding how to recognize problematic situations and address them. Being aware there's a problem is often trickier than fixing it, as dysfunctional behaviors can become entrenched in an organization's culture and then appear to be acceptable, not needing attention and change.

As the cover illustrates, this book offers nonprofit leaders a pathway out of the forest of confusing and stressful situations that frequently arise in our organizations.

The essays are divided into five sections:

➤ **Section I: The World of Nonprofits** includes general topics about nonprofits and how they operate

➤ **Section II: Nonprofit Operations and Excellence** covers management issues essential for high-performing nonprofits

➤ **Section III: Tips for Grant Makers and Grant Seekers** offers suggestions for grant makers as they work with nonprofits and for nonprofits in their interactions with funders

➤ **Section IV: Board Structure** covers topics about how to build and maintain a high performing board

➤ **Section V: Board Operations** offers specific suggestions for ensuring quality, strong volunteer leadership

A word of caution to board members reading this book: this isn't about becoming a board member from hell, identifying every small issue in a dictatorial or controlling way.
Rather, it's about:

➤ Realizing that a healthy, highly functional nonprofit board is *essential* for the survival of a nonprofit;

➤ Recognizing that board members have a responsibility to ensure they are successfully doing their jobs; and

➢ Having the courage to speak up when a problem is apparent and needs to be addressed.

So what's in this book for you, whether you are a board member, staff member, or a volunteer, are some topics that may get you thinking, "so *that's* what was going on when John did what he did" or, "we've got to change this," or "*that's* why I was so uncomfortable during that discussion." Hopefully you might also react to some essays with a "wow, what a great idea!" or, "I'm going to bring this up for discussion at the next board or staff meeting."

Likewise, if you are in a leadership position of a nonprofit organization it is our hope that this book of practical essays will provide you with helpful best practice tips that have been learned from many years working in the trenches with hundreds of nonprofit organizations and their leaders.

Please use this book as a catalyst to get the discussion going. In fact, feel free to blame it on the book!

PREFACE

Louis J. Beccaria, Ph.D.

My journey in the nonprofit sector began almost a half-century ago and every day has been a joy and a wonderful learning experience. From my days as a student at LaSalle College High School I felt drawn to community efforts to make the world a better place. I also took to heart my dad's words, who himself set the example by being very philanthropic with his time as a volunteer, when he counseled me "don't just take up space in life, make a difference." My singular purpose during my nonprofit sector professional journey has been to make a difference in the world and the community in which I live as well as to make my dad proud.

Besides being blessed with the very meaningful professional opportunity of working in the nonprofit field, I've been rewarded with the chance to meet many fine people who themselves are driven primarily by mission rather than money and are making a difference in their communities and/or in their chosen field of professional endeavor. They've shown time and again that the world is made up of many very good people whose sole interest is to improve the quality of life of their fellow citizens and the communities where they live.

With this as a backdrop, my motivation for co-authoring this book with Connie has been two-fold: to give back to the field that has treated me so well and provided me with the sense of ultimate professional fulfillment and to give mentoring counsel to those new to the nonprofit field as well as those veterans still toiling in the vineyard. While I shy away from the word "expert," I do consider myself knowledgeable with something to give back about the practice of philanthropy and nonprofit management.

It is my hope and prayer that those who read these pages written by Connie and me will feel that their time was well-spent, they will become more knowledgeable about best practices, and their professional careers will be enhanced by what they have read.

Constance Carter, CFRE

After working in the nonprofit world for decades, I have spent the last fifteen years running my own business, Sylvia & Carter & Associates, and as a result have had opportunities to learn about scores of nonprofit organizations, their boards, and staffs. I've seen missions flourish and organizations be incredibly successful; I have partnered with those trying to do better; and I've seen nonprofits struggle with dysfunction and survive – and sadly, a few that have failed.

Throughout the years I have noticed certain trends. Organizations that had robust, committed boards with flourishing standing committees, an open and transparent culture, and inspired executive leadership seemed to do well. They faced difficulties just like every other group, but they worked as a team and were resilient. Nonprofits with small, weak boards that were afraid of change and had tired, defeated executives who lacked the authority to lead their organizations struggled each and every day for survival. Some didn't make it.

Being an eternal optimist (coming from years of raising money), I thought if nonprofit leaders had some encouragement and a bit more knowledge, some of these problems could be solved or even avoided. Our nonprofits might grow stronger if we just learned how to recognize the symptoms, had the courage to address them, and some tools to craft solutions.

I hope you find some inspiration in this book, or an idea that suggests new possibilities or opportunities. You might find some new concepts to experiment with or strategies to consider. Or perhaps you'll experience confirmation that you're doing things well. And if that's the case, bravo!

ACKNOWLEDGEMENTS

There are many individuals we want to thank who helped make this literary journey possible and accompanied us along the way. We owe them debts of gratitude for their important roles in getting us across the finish line.

First of all, we would like to recognize all the nonprofit organizations and the many foundations we have worked and collaborated with over the past 50 years. They have given us the inspiration to share what we learned from them, and for giving us the opportunity to pass on what we have learned to others.

Secondly, we are very much in debt to Dr. Joseph D'Angelo, a long-term friend of Lou's (classmate at LaSalle College High School, Class of 1963). Using his extensive experience as a distinguished English professor and writer himself, he provided his valuable editing expertise in punctuation, grammar, and phrasing to make our manuscript more readable. We can only feel that our book would have suffered greatly without his input! We are also grateful for his thoughtful endorsement.

Warmhearted thanks also go to Connie's sister, Helene Sheeran, a key member of our editing team. Helene's eagle eye and focus on clarity significantly improved the essays. Her patience, willingness to help, encouragement, and critical skills are so appreciated and cherished.

We want to thank Marie Moss for contributing her graphic design skills and expertise in creating front and back covers that speak to the essence of our book's content and mission. Marie also skillfully guided us through the process of selecting images for the covers, totally new territory for us.

We are very grateful to Tish Mogan, Standards of Excellence Program Director of the Pennsylvania Association of Nonprofit Organizations, for the thoughtful and insightful Foreword she has contributed, and for her critique of the work as it progressed. We are extremely honored to have her imprimatur associated with this book.

Huge thanks go to Joe McKeever and Dave Carpenter who graciously allowed us to use their cartoons free of charge. Your generosity helps to lighten otherwise serious subjects, and for that we are very grateful!

To Karen Simmons, President and CEO of the Chester County Community Foundation, for her generous endorsement and for her visionary, thought-provoking work on behalf of the nonprofit community.

We also appreciate the endorsement from Kris Keller who is a dedicated student of best practices and a most valued and impactful nonprofit professional practicing in the Phoenixville area.

To Sr. Patricia Schnapp and June McInerney for their contributions of philanthropy poetry – not your typical subject for poetry -- and they rose to the challenge admirably.

To Avery Grace Beccaria, Lou's granddaughter, for lending her artistic skill at her tender age of 10 to creatively express the beautiful meaning of philanthropy.

To those whom we interviewed for the essay "Learning From Nonprofits and For-Profits": Rich Bevan, Brad Dunn, Rob Ellis, Anthony Gold, Bob Madonna, Anthony Odorisio, Lew Osterhoudt, Clemens Pietzner, John (Turk) Thacher, and Eva Verplanck, we share our joint gratitude for the time they gave us for the interviews and for their wisdom as experienced professionals who have traversed both the nonprofit and for-profit sectors.

Many thanks to Chris Golden for her expertise in finance and accounting and her careful review of the essay "The Critical Importance of Operating Reserves." With her stamp of approval, we are confident all is appropriate and accurate.

For the contribution of Clair Leaman, who printed this book, for his guidance and professionalism in turning our work into a finished, beautiful book.

To Corrine Sylvia, Connie's business partner at Sylvia & Carter & Associates, for her wisdom and savvy fundraising knowledge shared over the years to benefit scores of nonprofit organizations. Her comment "Campaigns fail due to lack of leadership, not due to lack of money" started us on our journey together and we've never looked back! Thank you.

To Lynn Seay, for her continuing emotional support, love, and patience as Lou worked to write and re-write his essays over many hours and months. With her clerical and internet technology skills, she helped Lou over his many computer barriers. For all this, he is very grateful.

To David Carter for accompanying Connie throughout this journey, offering his wisdom, experience, and insights resulting from decades of service to the nonprofit sector. David was always a thoughtful editor and contributor, frequently changing the order of bulleted items, and a steadfast admirer of the Oxford comma. For that, and so much more, my loving thanks to you.

How to Use This Book

Constance Carter

I am only one,
But still I am one.
I cannot do everything,
But still I can do something;
And because I cannot do everything
I will not refuse to do the something that I can do.

Edward Everett Hale

Many of the essays in this book are written from the perspective of an organization that has paid staff and a volunteer board of directors. However, we are aware many smaller, young, and/or grassroots nonprofits are run entirely by volunteers. In those organizations board members often fulfill the tasks typically assigned to staff, and the board assumes operational and policy-related responsibilities. Both are equally important.

All of these essays and a majority of the items in the appendix pertain to small and large nonprofits alike, with or without staff. Some may apply today, and some may function as inspirational concepts for the near or distant future. If your organization is all volunteer, we suggest that when reading an article that references the Executive Director or staff, simply think about the volunteers who fulfill those specific functions. Certainly, the relationships will be different, but most of the concepts regarding accountability, clear communication, and collaboration are very similar.

As an organization grows and its programs develop, the leadership needs to change. A founding board that previously delivered programs, wrote the checks, and raised the money may need to expand its network and gradually become more oriented to planning, relationship-building, and strategic thinking. Many of the essays in this book provide guidance about how to recognize and navigate these changes successfully.

It is our hope that this book will be a trusted guide as your organization grows.

Philanthropical funds are not lent.
Instead, they are generously spent
By philanthropists who, you will find,
Have genuine concern for all of mankind.
They give funds altruistically away to those with needs,
Charities and organizations which all do good deeds,
Striving to make the world a better place
For every member of our human race.

PART I: THE WORLD OF NONPROFITS

Philanthropy: The Broader View

Louis J. Beccaria

"There is no better exercise for your heart than reaching
Down and helping to lift someone up."
Bernard Meltzer

I would like to challenge you to think of philanthropy in a broad and philosophical or reflective way. The word *"philanthropy"* has a Greek root meaning "love of mankind," with *"phil"* meaning love and *"anthro"* meaning mankind. Traditionally, we've considered this term almost exclusively in a financial way to mean wealthy people giving money to help a valuable cause in which they have a particular interest. I'd like to offer a few thoughts to challenge you to consider other ways to think about philanthropy, and to practice the philanthropic spirit, with a wider perspective for the benefit of all.

Philanthropy is, in a deeper sense, the giving of something that has value to another person or organization. Aside from giving large amounts of money, people can donate smaller amounts and still be considered a philanthropist. These small amounts have value for both the giver and the receiver. Consider the act of dropping money in the collection box at a religious service, or the amounts that a caring child may raise via a special fundraising effort of selling lemonade or running laps around the block to help children afflicted with cancer. This effort has value; even the smaller amounts are valuable currency because these modest amounts, given by many people, have impact.

These two methods of giving money are typically how we think of practicing philanthropy. They are effective, even essential, and in their own way have impact on the causes they support.

A second way of practicing philanthropy is through *volunteering*. This is an age-old concept, but we often don't think of it as philanthropic. We merely feel that we're doing something good for another person or organization without being paid, and that is that!

When volunteering we're providing very valuable gifts – our time, our expertise, our knowledge, and our commitment and dedication to a cause. Many nonprofit organizations could not exist without this kind of philanthropy. It is so valuable, in fact, that many funders will ask a nonprofit organization that is requesting a grant how many hours of volunteer labor have been contributed in the past year to the organization. This contribution of "sweat equity" is not only valuable for the actual work being done but equally important for what it represents to the funder: broad community acceptance and appreciation of the organization. It goes a long way in the minds of potential funders to know that the requesting nonprofit group is so important to the community that individuals are willing to commit and dedicate their time, expertise, and knowledge to the cause.

A third and broader view of philanthropy involves the concepts of kindness and compassion. Most of us rarely think of acts of kindness and compassion as philanthropic. Yet we really should! Here's why.

When we go outside of ourselves and extend ourselves to be kind toward someone, we're practicing an aspect of philanthropic love in the truest sense. Webster's dictionary says that "kindness is the quality of being friendly, generous, and considerate." This entails showing, at some level, affection, gentleness, warmth, concern, and care.

Kindness requires only two essential elements: the awareness that kindness is important to show others and the will to do it. It can be almost effortless to demonstrate kindness. In fact, some scientists say that we're physiologically wired for it. Further, some believe that it's fundamental to our human existence and in our DNA framework to both need kindness and to give it.

As we go about our daily lives, we may not think about how extremely important and meaningful acts of philanthropic kindness can be for those on the receiving end of such acts. There are myriad examples of how we can show kindness.

Here are just a few examples:

- ➢ Saying "nice job" or "it looks good" while passing a custodian working in the hallway at a school or college who is probably on the low end of the economic and status level of that organization. He/she may rarely get a kind word about their work, maybe even from their own supervisor! We may forget that we all need and would like a little recognition and kindness shown our way once in a while. How often do we ever show this type of kindness?

- ➢ Sending someone flowers for no particular reason

- ➢ Bringing toys to children at a local homeless shelter

- ➢ Picking up litter at the local park

- ➢ Helping someone put their groceries in the car

- ➢ Shoveling the snow, without being asked, for an elderly neighbor

- ➢ Holding the elevator door for someone coming behind you

- ➢ There are many more examples that you could think of, I'm sure!

As Dr. Ethel Percy Andrus, founder of AARP, once wrote:

"It is only in the giving of oneself to others that we truly live".

Fourth, compassion is an even broader way to view philanthropy. Webster's dictionary defines compassion as "recognizing the suffering of others and then taking action to help." This embodies a tangible expression of love, indeed.

In a similar way as kindness, expressing compassion first takes a consciousness and awareness that someone is going through or has gone through some suffering in their life. As with kindness, expressing compassion requires taking action and getting involved in some way. It is not necessarily concerned with material or physical things. It is concerned with the human spirit and soul, as all love is.

Philanthropic compassionate love can be expressed on a personal, individual level or in a broader societal way such as social action or advocacy. Here are some examples of philanthropic compassionate love:

> Sharing a hug with someone who needs encouragement
> Saying some encouraging or uplifting words when someone is down
> Motivating someone who lacks confidence
> Sharing valuable time with someone to offer personal support
> Simply listening when someone needs to be heard
> Offering to help with a to-do list for someone who is struggling
> Getting involved in advocacy and speaking up for a cause relating to relieving hardships or suffering, such as elderly, child abuse, hunger, domestic violence prevention efforts, or homelessness programs.

This is being written during the tragic period of the COVID-19 virus. During this time, we have had myriad opportunities to learn about the dire world-wide need for more kindness and compassion in our personal and political lives.

Artist - Avery Grace Beccaria

Effective Philanthropic Leadership

Louis J. Beccaria

It cannot be overstated how important choosing the right Executive Director or CEO is for a nonprofit organization, foundation, or corporate philanthropy program. Whether an organization is brand new or has some years under its belt, there are certain qualities and characteristics that remain constant.

Based upon our experience on both sides of philanthropy (the nonprofit grant seeking side and the grant making side), it is evident to us that the following thirteen characteristics (in no particular priority order) are often found in the successful and effective leaders who populate the field, no matter what size their organization may be.

1. Having a Vision: A leader should be able to look broadly and long-range regarding the possibilities and opportunities open to the organization. A good leader must dream a little bit and see beyond the issues, problems, and resources of the present, articulating to all stakeholders (board, staff, volunteers, and funders) a guide or a roadmap that provides direction and excitement for the near or distant future.

2. Having a Passion for the Cause: It's absolutely essential to have that "fire in the belly" for the mission of the organization. This passion engenders creativity, sees one through the tough times when resources are scarce or other problems present themselves, and gives meaning to all the time, effort, and hard work employed. Likewise, it can be motivational for those around the leader, both inside and outside the organization, and can generate within them a similar sense of passion, excitement, and a quest for excellence in pursuit of the organization's mission.

3. Having a Passion for Achieving Excellence: Without the passion to achieve excellence in the pursuit of the organization's mission, a leader is merely a place-holder, marking time, punching a timeclock, and collecting a paycheck. The pursuit of excellence means trying to live up to high standards of best practices regarding program efficiency,

effectiveness, and impact as well as the best use of resources. Further, it means being serious about trying to make the organization, and those who comprise it, continually better tomorrow than today.

4. Being Ethically Grounded: Effective leadership is embodied in a leader who adheres to general societal moral standards as well as those of the philanthropy field. Some of the hallmarks of an ethical leader include the following:

*Honesty	*Sense of Community	*Veracity
*Justice	*Integrity	*Fidelity
*Respect	*Fairness	*Adherence
*Equity	*Compassion	to a set of
		values

Because of the inherent power dimension involved in the practice of both sides of philanthropy, (i.e., the grant seekers and the grant makers), the practice of these principles by the leaders of nonprofit organizations and the CEOs of foundations and corporate giving programs is absolutely crucial. (For more on this topic see "The Importance of Ethics" in Section I.)

5. Being a High Energy Person: Because there is a limited amount of time in which to pursue the organization's mission and, hopefully, seek that level of excellence mentioned above, a leader must demonstrate a high energy personality. It is this high energy that also spurs on creativity and can act as a role model for staff. As in any position, a nonprofit agency or philanthropy leader has a platform for only a limited time period in which to make a difference.

6. Having Excellent Recruiting Skills: Using a musical metaphor, an excellent leader is similar to an orchestra conductor. An orchestra conductor must recruit the best musical talent possible to play the various instruments required to make beautiful and harmonious music. So too, the leader of a nonprofit organization or a foundation has similar responsibilities.

Recruiting staff who fit well into the organization's group culture and its personal staff chemistry is critical in my judgment. Hiring staff who do not fit this profile can cause monumental issues and be like a cancer cell spreading like wildfire. Likewise, hiring people who have expertise in their area of responsibility, along with a great work ethic and passion for the cause are essential for the organization to perform effectively and in harmony.

Being able to choose talent well is a major aspect of outstanding leadership. This goes a very long way in helping the organization accomplish its mission. Also, it is essential that the Executive Director or CEO embrace the maxim that a fine leader hires people who are smarter in their area of responsibility than the leader is. This requires keeping one's ego in check for the sake of the organization and its effectiveness.

7. Being Well Organized: Using one's time well, being able to set priorities, and do necessary follow-up allow many of the other qualities mentioned here to flourish. It also can set an example for staff who are constantly looking at the organization's leader (whether he/she knows it or not) as a role model! Being well-organized also ensures the efficient use of available resources. When one is well-organized, resources such as time, collaboration with others, and money can be utilized more efficiently and effectively.

8. Following Through on Commitments: Nothing can detract from a leader's credibility more than not following through on commitments no matter how large or small they may be. This quality speaks loudly about the leader's personality and reliability. There is no better way for a leader to lose his or her trust among staff, board, and the community-at-large than to get a reputation for offering hollow promises that are not kept. Besides showing respect for staff, board, and the community, following through shows dedication to the task at hand and is emblematic of a person who has a "can do" attitude and reputation.

9. Being Able to Think Outside the Box: In the ever-changing world in which we live, a leader needs to be reflective and show adaptability and flexibility to these changing circumstances. The ability to solve different issues in varied situations is dependent on these qualities. Old ways of thinking that may have worked in the past no longer may be effective.

Investigating new ways to solve problems/issues and seeking new ways of using ever more-scarce human, program, and financial resources, and finding alternative solutions and options are critically important. Researching best practices is one way of doing this.

Being reflective and thinking in new, out-of-the-box ways often can spell the success or failure of the leader. In the years ahead, because of the massive societal changes brought on by the growth and importance of technology, and the impact of the post-pandemic environment, being a reflective leader who looks for more efficient ways to be effective and impactful will be an increasingly critical leadership quality.

10. Keeping One's Ego in Check: While the Executive Director or CEO is the top person in the organization's hierarchy, this does not mean that the organization is this person's fiefdom. To use a common term: "It's not all about her or him." The good and effective leader must remember that no one achieves any amount of success in today's world alone or without the efforts and talents of others in the organization. To paraphrase a well-known saying: "It takes a village to successfully manage an organization."

In this sense it takes humility and a sense of gratitude on the part of the leader to say "thank you," or "you did a good job on that," or "we couldn't have accomplished this without your expertise and dedication." Comments such as these, and others, go a long way in building support for the organization's leader among staff at all levels, and the organization as a whole benefits in the long run.

11. Being a Good Networker: Casting a net to develop relationships is an increasingly important characteristic of an effective leader. It is often through networking that serendipitous things happen in the pursuit of the organization's mission. Networking can lead to locating new funding sources, identifying needed staff, finding good board members, uncovering a fruitful collaborative opportunity in the community, coming up with a new idea, or having support/resource persons in the wings to help answer questions and solve issues. There really is no downside to networking. The only requirement is for the leader to be open to it.

12. Thinking "Team": An effective and successful leader must have an inclusive mentality in today's world and must understand that it takes a team of people to accomplish an organization's mission.

For example, every person in the organization has an important role to play no matter their place in the organization's hierarchy or their pay grade, be they the CEO, program director, case manager, food service employee, maintenance person, executive assistant, or other support persons. They are in the organization for a reason. They all have value, and they need to be recognized for that value. Often the people at the lower end of the organizational hierarchy have the best ideas for resolving issues. The leader needs to listen to them.

The athletic metaphor of "team" is not a stretch when trying to make this point. "There is no "I" in "Team"! When a leader is secure enough to be a servant leader and share recognition and credit for accomplishments, everyone in the organization benefits.

13. Being Open to Learning: I know of an outstanding leader whose motto was: "When we stop getting better, we stop being good." This is just another way of saying that a leader must be open to learning new ways of doing things in the pursuit of the organization's mission. There are often new theories, new approaches, and methodologies that potentially can be employed for the good of the organization. Good leaders must be open to considering and evaluating new knowledge presented to them. What worked yesterday may not work today.

In short, the organization's leader must be the "culture captain," leading their nonprofit organization or foundation to becoming a "learning" organization.

CHANGING THE NONPROFIT
"VOW OF POVERTY" MENTALITY

Constance Carter

"Well, since you both have taken vows of poverty, I'm not surprised you aren't interested in discussing a creative for-profit strategy that would spin off income to fund your nonprofit." The construction supervisor for our building project stepped back and waited for his words to sink in. The Executive Director and I looked at each other, and said, "Vows of poverty? Us?"

We thought we were managing things pretty well. Sure, we scrimped and saved and used both sides of every piece of paper, had old computers that were powered by gerbils, and worked in offices that were tucked under stairwells, in closets, and old elevator shafts, but that's life in a nonprofit, right? What's wrong with that? *That's just the way it is.*

After many decades of working in nonprofit fundraising and management, I have finally seen that his words were true. Through no fault of our own, most of us working in nonprofits today have taken vows of poverty, often without even knowing it. And while a vow of poverty might be highly acceptable and even admirable in religious life, there are many factors that indicate it does not serve the nonprofit sector well.

Dan Pallotta, author of <u>Charity Case</u>, stated in his September 14, 2012 *Wall Street Journal* article *Why Can't We Sell Charity Like We Sell Perfume?:*

"In short, we are asking nonprofit groups to deal with social problems whose scale is beyond easy comprehension, while denying those groups the tools they need to build any meaningful scale themselves."

What Do Nonprofits Do?

Nonprofit organizations today provide food, medical and dental care, housing, daycare, mental health services, substance abuse prevention, education, and senior care for our communities, and much more, that America's safety net does not. In the last 30 to 40 years, nonprofit organizations have taken the place of programs previously funded by the government, as well as many that were run by religious organizations.

Nonprofit organizations also supplement the role of government programs that are no longer sufficiently funded. For example, consider the federal food stamp program SNAP (Supplemental Nutrition Assistance Program), which typically only provides for three weeks of food per month. Food cupboards, food banks, and community and faith-based organizations, most of them nonprofit organizations, step in and provide families with food for that crucial last week of the month.

Nonprofits frequently have higher standards and provide services of equal or greater quality than some of their for-profit colleagues. Healthcare organizations that serve low-income individuals on Medicaid, which usually pays only 50-60% of the cost of providing care, are excellent examples. Revenues generated by fundraising (an income stream available only to nonprofit organizations) bridge the gap between the actual cost of providing services and the Medicaid reimbursements.

The nonprofit sector does more than meet our basic needs. Consider the wide range of arts, culture, historic preservation, advocacy, environmental, animal welfare, and educational organizations that enrich our quality of life. Most are nonprofit. And nonprofit organizations are now being formed to cope with funding cuts for libraries and public schools that previously were entirely funded by government sources.

Thus, despite their challenges, nonprofit organizations have created a culture of excellence. We rely on them to meet basic needs; to enlighten, inspire, and educate us; and to provide a voice for those who lack one. Where did this "vow of poverty" ethic come from?

The Vow of Poverty

The vow of poverty concept in the western world stems from centuries of strong traditions of religious sects that, before the government stepped in, provided many of the services nonprofit organizations do today. Members of these groups actually took vows of poverty. Priests, nuns, and missionaries received little or no pay and had limited or no personal property. Their lives were dedicated to this work, which was viewed as service to God. The care provided was considered charity.

Today, the vow of poverty ethic is engrained in many people who are attracted to working and volunteering for nonprofit organizations, whether or not they are or have been affiliated with a religious organization. During my long career in the nonprofit world I've frequently heard (and said) comments like:

> ➤ *"I don't mind a low salary. I know I'm helping people."*
> ➤ *"Changing people's lives for the better is more important than having a pension."*
> ➤ *"I have a reason to get up in the morning and that motivates me, not the paycheck."*
> ➤ *"I don't need a new computer; we serve poor people here."*

The vow of poverty syndrome often looks like fiscal responsibility and dedication to serving the poor. Thus, nonprofits allocate most of their financial resources to their programs. Ensuring that staff members are fairly compensated and have the resources they need to do their jobs efficiently and effectively is not a priority. Leaders believe that their organization and its employees are less important than the clients they serve. This short-sighted attitude makes it difficult for staff members to ask for what they need as the focus is outward, on the mission. The work ethic is "we can make do." And, despite what organization's leaders may think, this approach does not serve clients well.

What's the Evidence?

It is easy to see the disparity between the for-profit and nonprofit sectors. Where else would you find outdated, slow computers that routinely break down? Inadequate, obsolete software? Mailing lists of thousands of names in an Excel spreadsheet or even a shoebox instead of an efficient database? Outmoded kitchens and poor restroom facilities? Third-hand equipment ready to be trashed? Our nonprofit can use it!

On the human resources side, pay scales and benefits are generally a fraction of those in the for-profit sector. Limited continuing education budgets and extremely long hours make it hard for nonprofit organizations to hire and retain experienced and visionary staff. Nonprofits offer low pay in return for demanding excellent work. The attitude of scarcity and lack negatively impacts motivation and creativity for both paid staff and volunteers. After doing a regional salary survey, one of my clients informed me that the only other CEO who had a salary less than hers was a nun - who received no pay at all.

This attitude is also evident in the reluctance of many nonprofit organizations to provide continuing education and growth opportunities for staff. Investing in human resources is an excellent way to keep people engaged, motivated, and current in their professions. Yet a typical nonprofit approach is "find a free workshop" or "you'll have to raise the money in order to pay for it." When the budget is tight, staff training is one of the first line items cut.

Dan Pallotta also stated in his article:

"We tend to think that policing salaries of charitable groups is an ethical imperative, but for would-be leaders, it results in a mutually exclusive choice between doing well for yourself and doing good for the world—and it causes many of the brightest kids coming out of college to march directly into the corporate world."

Evidence of this can also be seen in uninspired, inexperienced board members who joined the board of directors not because they have professional skills to offer and a passion for the work of the organization but because "someone asked me to join and said anyone can do it." The vow of poverty syndrome also crushes motivation among the leadership. Nonprofit leaders are often stretched to their limits laboring with inadequate resources for funding, staff, volunteers, equipment, and facilities. They rarely have a chance to try new ideas, be creative, and take risks. Often, their initiative is further limited by constraints requiring them to "check with the board" before trying new approaches.

Let's Change the Thinking

The Minnesota Council on Nonprofits defines nonprofit organizations:

"Nonprofit organizations, also known as charitable organizations, tax-exempt organizations, or non-governmental organizations, are organizations, or corporate entities, that are formed for the purpose of fulfilling a mission to improve the common good of society rather than to acquire and distribute profits. The defining feature of nonprofit organizations is that they do not distribute a financial return (equity), or profit, to private individuals. Instead, a nonprofit utilizes any profits in service to the public interest, i.e. to fulfill the nonprofit's mission."

Does the term "nonprofit" set us up for our vow of poverty and a self-limiting mentality? In a way, despite the definition above, the term implies we're not allowed to make money.

Dan Pallotta noted:

"Self-deprivation is our strategy for social change. The dysfunction at the heart of our approach is neatly captured by our narrow, negative label for the charitable sector: 'not-for-profit'."

The term also implies that losing money is acceptable or even expected. After all, that's not making a profit, right? Many times, in my consulting work I'm asked by an organization, "Is it OK for us to make a profit at the end of the year? That's bad, right? After all, we're a nonprofit."

The truth is that breaking even or making a profit at the end of the year are evidence of strong fiscal leadership, not irresponsible excess. (For more on this topic see the article "The Critical Importance of Operating Reserves" in Section II.)

The word charity is also problematic. The term is reminiscent of the workhouses, orphanages, and institutions of the Dickensian era. Today, organizations that qualify with the Internal Revenue Service as tax-exempt must achieve and maintain "public charity status." The word charity in this context is even more loaded with unsuccessful and un-businesslike values than the word nonprofit.

Dan Pallotta further notes:

"It's time to change how society thinks about charity and social reform. The donating public is obsessed with restrictions—nonprofits shouldn't pay executives too much, or spend a lot on overhead, or take risks with donated dollars. **It should be asking whether these organizations have what they need to actually solve problems.** *The conventional wisdom is that low costs serve the higher good. But this view is killing the ability of nonprofits to make progress against our most pressing problems. Long-term solutions require investment in things that don't show results in the short term."*

Examining how we describe ourselves is the first step to changing how we see ourselves.

Curtis Klotz in the August 2019 <u>Nonprofit Quarterly</u> article titled: *"A Graphic Revisioning of Nonprofit Overhead"* notes that *"Strategic financial functions, good governance, and the development of key funding partnerships are vital to strong organizations ... Rather than thinking of our investment in key infrastructure as diminishing our programs, it should be seen as valuable Core Mission Support."*

Suggestions for Making Change

Invest in the infrastructure (equipment/technology/resources).
Give staff members the tools they need to do their jobs efficiently and effectively. Banish donated laptops with Windows 95, slow Internet connections, and telephone systems without voicemail or that drop calls.

Invest in the paid staff.
Spend enough to recruit and retain qualified, capable people. Nonprofit leaders are often paid far less than their for-profit or government

colleagues and receive poor benefits. Nonprofits do exceptionally vital work. They should benefit from high-quality professionals who are experts in their fields.

Train the staff you have.
Invest in staff development. Help staff members stay current and motivated in their professions. Learn from successful for-profit businesses known for being good places to work. For example, how many nonprofit organizations provide rewards for staff who develop new ideas and initiatives or reach certain goals?

Invest in the board of directors.
The nonprofit board of directors is charged not only with fiduciary and legal oversight for the organization but also responsibility for raising funds and ensuring the mission is being achieved. Carefully select board members for their commitment to the mission, their professional skills, and their dedication to promote the organization effectively. The board should be provided the training and resources it needs in order to be effective. The board should also monitor and evaluate itself to ensure it is doing its job. *This is too important to leave to happenstance.*

Invest in the facilities.
Nonprofits do very important work, which should be done in facilities that serve the mission, not where people have to constantly adapt to fit the facilities. Leaky roofs, inadequate security, and offices in depressing run-down buildings, basements, and trailers are unacceptable.

How do we pay for this investment?
A recent article from the National Council on Nonprofits states:
"Enlightened donors and grantmakers recognize that administrative costs are essential in order for charitable nonprofits to be <u>financially sustainable,</u> but for too long, "overhead" has gotten a bad rap and been inappropriately used as a measure of a nonprofit's effectiveness. The assumption that overhead is "bad" reflects a mis-appreciation of the reality of what it costs to deliver a nonprofit's mission."

Ensure the organization is providing top-quality programs that really work.
Invest in evaluating (and if needed, improving) the effectiveness of programs so you can *prove* to donors that the organization is doing what it says it does and is truly making a difference. Learn how to measure and document your outcomes.

Invest in promoting the organization.
The for-profit equivalent of fundraising is marketing and sales. We know that for-profit businesses invest in these activities because *they bring in revenue.* This is a basic concept that drives the for-profit sector, and this idea needs to become part of nonprofit values and practices as well.

Educate the board of directors about their roles as fundraisers.
Teach board members how to successfully raise money. There are many different ways board members can help promote the organization and raise money beyond asking someone outright, which is usually the primary fear board members have. Like staff, board members need to be provided with tools and support in order to be successful.

Build an effective fundraising department.
Hire capable, experienced staff members and/or consultants. Develop a strong, self-respecting attitude as to how the nonprofit changes lives and deserves support and investment. Change the "gift, charity, or donation" mentality to one of seeking "investment" in the organization's work and the opportunity to make a difference in it. Because fundraising is not direct services, it is often last in line when creating a budget.

Be willing to pay for training, consulting services, and other supplemental tools that will build the skills of staff and increase their productivity … and as a result, their job satisfaction and the organization's success.

Next Steps

Here are a few suggestions:

1. Ask if you are mired in a vow of poverty. Do you promote it at your organization? Might you instead be willing to take the risk and envision a more generative, abundant operating system to enable nonprofits to flourish and grow?

2. Think about how the vow of poverty relates to your nonprofit experiences—as a staff member, board member, funder, volunteer, consultant, or client—what resonates for you?

3. Discuss this article with your colleagues. Ask if they have seen examples of the vow of poverty themselves, and what their experiences have been.

4. Review this article with your board. Ask them to consider the concepts. Engage them in open, honest discussions about how your nonprofit organization operates.

5. Explore with others how change could occur. Take the risk to think about the nonprofit organization, its work, and its clients, and discuss how you might do things differently and more successfully for your mission and your organization.

6. Change the organizational culture of your nonprofit organization by being mindful about the language employed in how board, staff, volunteers, and others refer to the organization.

7. If possible, and you have the courage, try and educate donors and funders that funding infrastructure and overhead expenses is vital to ensuring the organization's survival and growth. As **Curtis Klotz** noted in the Nonprofit Quarterly article, *"When funders support only direct expenses, they deny funding for Core Mission Support. This leaves a gap at the center of our organization. Not only is one program affected, but the health of the entire organization is at risk."*

Learning from Nonprofits and For-Profits

Louis J. Beccaria and Constance Carter

"I've been an assassin for the CIA, a hit man for the mob, and a freelance killer. But I've never sunk so low as to be a corporate board member."
from a novel by Stuart Woods

The above words, spoken by ex-CIA operative Teddy Fay, aptly summarize the attitude many people have about the for-profit sector. People involved with nonprofits often consider the for-profit world to be without morals or ethics, driven by the bottom line, and symbolizing all that's negative about doing business. Those in the for-profit sector frequently look condescendingly at nonprofits, citing their lack of business acumen and poor management, often commenting, "Well, what can you expect, after all, it's a nonprofit."

The differences between for-profits and nonprofits can become challenging when former for-profit workers or retirees become nonprofit board or committee members, volunteers, or staff. Board members from the for-profit sector may assume a similar culture exists in a nonprofit, and without some guidance and mentoring, may have difficulty managing their expectations and assumptions. One nonprofit executive commented, "Board members, especially those from for-profit businesses, need to be provided with comprehensive training to fully educate them about the organization and its culture. It takes time for this learning to evolve and most organizations rush through it, leaving new board members unprepared."

Understanding and respecting the differences between the for-profit and nonprofit sectors is essential to building productive relationships. Here are some comments about frequently-encountered cultural differences and suggestions for ways to navigate this challenging territory. The comments in italics are compiled from interviews with corporate executives who have nonprofit experience, either as staff or volunteers.

Small to mid-size nonprofits may have more success recruiting board members from similar-sized, local for-profit businesses than from large corporations.

The cultural differences between the nonprofit and for-profit sectors vary significantly depending on the size of the organizations. The cultural divide between corporate finance and a nonprofit bare-bones budget that's dependent on donations is significant and may be too wide to navigate. Nonprofits are often attracted to recruiting high-powered executives because of their prestige, name recognition, community visibility, and respect. However, many of these CEOs have little time for board meetings and even less for extra activities, such as networking, making introductions, or attending planning sessions and events.

One nonprofit CEO commented, "Changing gears from a large for-profit business to a smaller nonprofit organization can be very difficult; the resources and pace are so different. In a small or mid-size organization board members need to be generalists, and they have to adapt their expertise and expectations to the needs and capacity of the nonprofit. Strategies that work in a large for-profit corporation may not work in a smaller nonprofit."

Executives from large corporations have more difficulty relating to the realities of a nonprofit with a $500,000 annual budget than a leader from a similar-sized company or family-owned business who may embody an entrepreneurial spirit that would fit well in a nonprofit. Furthermore, leaders from local businesses often have a vested interest in the health and success of the community's nonprofit sector, as their employees and customers may live nearby.

Nonprofits should not be designed or allowed to run in the red or lose money.

There is no excuse for poor financial management. One for-profit bank executive felt it was acceptable for his nonprofit organization to have an annual deficit because "it showed they needed support." As a result, he and the rest of the board ignored years of poor financial management that drained their financial reserves, cost them donor support, and threatened to close the organization.

It is essential for nonprofits to build reserve funds of nine months or more of operating expenses. These reserves will protect the organization from financial fluctuations such as losing a major donor, a reduction in government funding, or a significant unexpected expense. (For more on this topic, see the article "The Critical Importance of Operating Reserves" in section II.)

Nonprofit board and staff need to pay ongoing and careful attention to budgets and finance reports. One executive noted, "Careful budgeting is life or death! This must be done thoughtfully and realistically." Establish systems and policies if there are none or strengthen them if they are ineffective. Provide training to empower and educate staff, board and committee members so they understand how to read financial reports and ask appropriate questions.

"It's good enough for a nonprofit" or "our clients aren't paying anyway so it's OK" are not acceptable justifications for poor quality work or performance.

Success in a for-profit corporation looks very different from success in a nonprofit organization. For-profits are in the business of making money for stockholders. Nonprofits are in the business of meeting community needs and solving problems, changing the world, and hopefully breaking even or making a modest profit. It's essential that for-profit board members learn and understand what success looks like in nonprofit organizations, and not evaluate them with the same criteria used in their corporations.

Nonprofits should routinely conduct evaluations and surveys to assess the quality and effectiveness of their work, periodically utilizing outside objective evaluators. Evaluations can help determine if the programs are effective, continuing to meet a demand, or if changes are needed. Organizations that refuse to adapt to changing community needs often face difficulty with fund raising, volunteer recruitment, and ultimately, survival. Evaluations will also be useful in developing outcomes for donors and funders, an increasingly essential component of successful fundraising initiatives. Providing training for the board and staff regarding program assessments and how to utilize evaluation data to improve programs will also be helpful.

A for-profit retiree noted, "In nonprofits accountability is not tied as closely to performance as in the for-profit world. There's no economic driver, such as bonuses or large pay raises, so the motivation for excellence has to come from someplace else."

Motivation starts with the Board of Directors and the Executive Director. Nonprofits offer meaningful opportunities for people to dedicate their lives to causes they care deeply about and to feel they have a mission or purpose. One executive who became a nonprofit leader observed that the staff actually liked their jobs, and she felt there was greater job satisfaction. "People work here for more than the paycheck," she reflected.

A nonprofit CEO noted, "Life is sometimes happier in a nonprofit. People are committed to their work and that's inspiring. However, it's also challenging because you see the real problems you're trying to address and that can be overwhelming, creating job stress and burnout. And most nonprofits don't have the resources to really support their staff."

Working in the nonprofit sector generally does not include stock options, six-figure bonuses, corporate jets, or lavish expense accounts. However, even though most nonprofit staff members get the intangible benefits of knowing they're doing good work and thereby deriving deep personal satisfaction from their careers, that's no excuse for substandard pay, benefits, and working conditions. Nonprofit professionals should not be required to "take a vow of poverty" or forgo building a 401K. Salaries and benefits need to be sufficient so the sector can attract and retain high quality talent.

One nonprofit Executive Director who was a career engineer commented, "There were lots of resources available within my company to help me solve problems. Telling a staff member to 'just figure a problem out' or 'just do it' may not work in a nonprofit as there may not be any help available."

Most nonprofits generally don't have access within their organizations to the same quantity or quality of resources that are available in for-profit businesses. Single or two-person departments are frequently the norm, not the exception. Sometimes hiring outside experts is the most efficient and cost-effective way to make progress. Board members and donors should respect and support this.

Nonprofits need to learn from the for-profit concept that it's appropriate to spend money to make money. "You can't cut your way to success," one executive commented. "Furthermore, if you're starving yourself, how can you be healthy?"

One executive who became a nonprofit Executive Director was shocked to see that staff had been struggling for years using outdated, slow computers that lacked current software. He commented, "I can't even begin to estimate the time that was being wasted, not to mention the frustration the staff experienced. I spent a few thousand dollars and bought everyone refurbished computers with the needed software. It literally turned the place around."

Here's another example of misplaced nonprofit frugality. A nonprofit was seeking a $500,000 capital campaign grant from a foundation located 1,000 miles away. Upon discussing this with their campaign committee, which comprised for-profit executives, the staff were shocked when the committee members suggested visiting the foundation. "But that will cost $1,000 in air fare," the Executive Director said. "Do the math," the committee members said. "Can't you spend $1,000 to make $500,000? Talk about return on investment!" They did, and they got the grant.

One thoughtful for-profit executive commented, "The for-profit attitude of 'everyone's replaceable, and if you can't/won't do it we'll find someone else who will' doesn't apply in a nonprofit. Also, nonprofits tend to value the concept of work/life balance, which is a refreshing difference." Another noted, "In my corporation there was tremendous pressure to produce, regardless of the human cost; the focus was exclusively on making a profit. In a nonprofit, the focus is on the people and the mission – it's a huge difference."

Because staff are compensated less in the nonprofit sector, boards and management can't expect staff to embrace the ethic of "I'll work as much as needed to get the job done," or put in 70 to 80-hour work weeks for no additional pay. And, because nonprofits are frequently understaffed due to budgetary restraints, the concept of "work smarter not harder" may not apply. The staff may already be doing the best they can with limited resources.

Another director commented, "In the for-profit culture there's tremendous pressure to get the work done and meet the deadline, whatever it takes, regardless of the toll that takes on the staff. Sometimes there's a slower pace in a nonprofit, and the more relaxed atmosphere is nice."

This slower pace, especially regarding decision-making, may frustrate a high-powered board or committee member from a for-profit corporation who is used to change occurring rapidly in a hierarchical way, versus the more time-consuming collaborative approach embraced by many nonprofits. It's important for nonprofit staff to be aware these differences may exist and provide appropriate coaching for new volunteers while also recognizing that some of the for-profit perspective and efficiency may be extremely helpful.

One retired for-profit executive who joined the staff of a nonprofit noted that because nonprofits aren't driven by a profit mentality, there was more flexibility and opportunities to take risks and try new things; there was a greater tolerance for failure. He observed this approach offered greater job satisfaction for staff who wanted to grow and learn.

This approach can be productive and create a positive work atmosphere, but it needs to be managed carefully. Sometimes a sense of urgency may be required to respond to a crisis or accomplish a challenging project, such as capital campaign or launching a new program. This requires teamwork, flexibility, and an ability to adapt. In those situations, advice and a nudge from the for-profit sector may be just what is needed.

One Executive Director new to the nonprofit world noted, "I found that I had to build collaborations and consensus with the goal of getting everyone to commit to an idea, vs. just telling them what they had to do. For me that was much more satisfying than my career as a for-profit manager, but it took a lot of learning, patience, time, and effort."

Successful nonprofit managers use a more collegial team-building management strategy vs. the autocratic, top-down style often found in for-profit businesses. Board members from the for-profit world need to respect different management approaches in order to effectively support the Executive Director. High performing nonprofit organizations benefit from strong, mutually-respectful relationships between the board and the Executive Director, and from a staff that functions as a supportive team.

Nonprofits need to embrace the value of spending time and money on strategic planning.

One retired executive who had specialized in corporate "turnarounds" for struggling businesses noted that successful for-profits and nonprofits provided services that were in demand. He also noted that it was important that nonprofits periodically examine what they were doing and how they did it, to determine if they were still relevant. He commented, "In the corporate world we spent time carefully studying problems before making decisions; it was time well spent. Sometimes it's important to step back and take a fresh look at everything."

Strategic planning provides nonprofits structured opportunities for thoughtful discussion and reflection among staff, volunteers, and others in the community. It is a time to review, evaluate, and consider new information and different approaches to old and new challenges. An annual review of the strategic plan to assess progress is another way to pause and reflect about the nonprofit's work.

Strategies to Consider

1. When recruiting a for-profit executive, be sure to educate the prospect about the work the nonprofit does, its culture, and how it operates. This is especially important if the prospect works in a large corporation. Conversations with other board members about how the board functions, site visits to the nonprofit to see the work in action (if appropriate), and a meeting with the Executive Director can all be helpful.

2. Thoroughly vetting prospective board members communicates the message that board membership is an important honor, and something the organization takes seriously. One for-profit executive commented, "Not only does vetting help to ensure the right fit, but it also creates a sense of demand or exclusivity. For nonprofits that will accept anyone as board members, there can be a sense of 'meh, why join, they'll take anyone who's breathing?'"

3. Enlist an existing board member to mentor and coach the new member for at least six months, answer questions, and debrief after each meeting. This also reinforces the concept that board membership is a serious job requiring training and support.

4. The board Chair should ensure discussions are thoughtful and respectful, and encourage members to ask questions, challenge assumptions, and suggest new approaches to old problems. Being open to different ways of thinking and working will help board members to feel comfortable sharing their expertise, even if the ideas are "out of the box."

5. All board members should feel comfortable holding the nonprofit accountable, especially regarding finances, deadlines, and essential reports. "It's just a nonprofit" is no excuse!

The Importance of Ethics

Constance Carter

"Ethics must begin at the top of an organization. It is a leadership issue and the chief executive must set the example."
Edward Hennessy, Philanthropist and Retired CEO

Nonprofit organizations must operate from an ethical framework or foundation. This is due to two fundamental elements of trust:

1) Nonprofits rely on **the public's trust**. This trust is essential in order to raise money, obtain government grants and contracts, and maintain a positive reputation. A donor must be able to trust that an organization will use his or her gift appropriately, whether cash or property, large or small.

2) Nonprofits are also entrusted with significant **responsibilities**. They are often responsible for:

> ➢ Caring for others (such as healthcare, daycares and schools, organizations serving low-income and/or vulnerable people, animal welfare),
> ➢ Promoting and supporting issues that affect many or all of us (the environment, civil liberties, religious institutions, voting rights), and
> ➢ Cultural treasures belonging to individuals and the public (museums, historical and cultural organizations).

In fact, today a nonprofit's ethics are considered to be so critically important that the IRS 990 (the tax form most nonprofits submit annually) contains several pages of ethically-focused questions about nepotism, lobbying, fiscal oversight, conflict of interest, transparency, and a variety of other business practices. Nepotism, lobbying, and other similar practices may be the norm in for-profit businesses; in nonprofits such behavior is considered a cause for concern.

Values Lead to Ethics

Ethics are different than values. Values are learned and/or chosen beliefs regarding what constitutes right and wrong behavior. ***Ethics are a manifestation or application of values***. Thus, ethical motivation is the desire to act and live in a manner consistent with one's values. This is why nonprofit organizations develop values statements. Organizations are motivated and expected to implement their missions consistent with their values, and those values provide the guidance and structure for making ethical decisions. Values statements clearly document the principles and beliefs that guide the activities of the overall organization: its board, staff, and volunteers. They provide a snapshot about how the nonprofit operates, motivate its donors and volunteers to donate their resources or time, and assist in recruiting staff.

Values are typically developed by the organization's founders and leaders. They must be lived and kept alive, vibrant, and contemporary by the current board, staff, and other stakeholders. Everyone involved with the nonprofit needs to be in basic agreement regarding their meaning and how they are interpreted. Here are some tips about how to keep values front and center:

> ➢ Read the mission and values at every board and staff meeting; include them in the agendas;
> ➢ All activities and decisions must reflect the values in some way;
> ➢ Post them on the website, social media, and key publications; and
> ➢ Review values statements periodically, as they may need to be changed or updated. This must be thoughtfully and collectively done by all stakeholders, not only the board, since all stakeholders are important. Be sure to examine the motives and reasons for change thoroughly before implementing them.

Ethics: An Extension of Values

Nonprofits need to adopt and maintain updated policies that support ethical leadership and management, such as:

> ➢ Personnel policies that can help avoid and/or resolve conflicts;

- ➢ Clearly stated grievance procedures; and
- ➢ Whistle-blower and conflict of interest policies.

Ethics violations can occur due to crimes of **commission**, such as when a person or organization intentionally behaves in an unethical way, or simply through acts of **omission,** such as not supervising people carefully enough, or a board not paying close enough attention to how the organization is operating. Placing too much trust in an individual or system without implementing checks and balances can lead to either of these situations.

One example of a Board of Directors not paying enough attention was Goodwill Omaha, which in 2016 was found, through a series of articles by an Omaha newspaper, to be paying executive staff inappropriately high salaries (some receiving $1 million or more) while workers with disabilities were paid less than minimum wage. This was particularly egregious and contrary to Goodwill's explicit and implicit values and mission because Goodwill was established as a champion of disadvantaged people struggling to get into the workforce.

As a result of this investigation, questions were also raised about nepotism and conflicts of interest at the board level. Ultimately, the CEO and some board members left the organization as donors became concerned and stopped giving, and the Nebraska Attorney General began an investigation. The board then worked to turn the organization around, starting with a top-to-bottom assessment, including an ethics review.

Conflict of Interest
A conflict of interest is a situation in which a person or organization is involved in multiple interests, financial or otherwise, one of which could possibly corrupt the ethical motivation or decision-making of that individual or organization. Properly handled, a potential conflict of interest can be discovered and voluntarily defused before any problems occur. Frequently people aren't aware that a conflict of interest may exist in a certain situation. To them, and perhaps others, it appears to be normal and not a problem. In fact, those involved may have never even considered the possibility that there could be an issue.

That is why it is so important for nonprofits to become vigilant about potential conflicts of interest, or even the appearance or possible perception that a conflict may be occurring. *It can't be managed properly if people don't know it's a possibility.* All high performing nonprofits should have a conflict of interest policy with written annual disclosures completed by board members and management staff. The disclosures should include any possible issues, jobs, memberships, or relationships that exist or may exist that could present conflicts of interest for the organization.

For example, a board member may own a building and rent space to the nonprofit. This could be a potential conflict of interest, especially if the rent was higher for the nonprofit than for others, or if the board member gained some other benefits. However, the conflict might be defused if:

> ➤ The situation was clearly disclosed to the rest of the board;
> ➤ The rent was fair market value or less; and
> ➤ The board member recused him/herself from the decision-making discussions.

Setting the Tone: Ethical Leadership
Being an ethical leader means going beyond being a good person. Ethical leaders make ethics a clear and consistent part of their agendas, set standards, model appropriate behavior, and hold everyone accountable. It's important for staff and volunteer leaders to make ethical culture a basis for everything that occurs in the organization. This involves constantly being on the lookout for potential conflicts of interest, regardless of where they occur – board, staff, donors, volunteers, or even clients.

Ethical leadership comprises three major elements:

> ➤ **Be the Example:** Actions often speak louder than words. People are more likely to judge someone based on how they act, rather than what they say. By practicing and demonstrating ethical, honest, and unselfish behavior to others, ethical leaders will earn

respect. People are more likely to follow a leader who respects others and shows integrity.

➤ **Promote the Importance of Ethics:** Ethical leaders focus on the overall importance of ethics and how these factors can influence the organization and society as a whole. As an ethical leader, it is important to teach others about ethics, especially in cases where they are faced with a challenging issue in the organization.

➤ **Communicate:** Successful ethical leaders tend to be good communicators. People communicate in different ways, and an effective leader is aware of this and continually works on it.

Justifying Unethical Behavior

There are many ways well-meaning and caring people can talk themselves into thinking unethical behavior is acceptable in a particular situation. Here are just a few:

➤ It's perfectly legal.
➤ Everyone else does it.
➤ It's all for a good cause.
➤ It's all part of the job.
➤ No one is getting hurt.
➤ This is a one-time exception.
➤ I deserve it.
➤ No one will find out.
➤ The ends justify the means.

If you catch yourself or anyone else in your organization making comments such as these, that could be a red flag that an ethics violation is looming. Quickly take the necessary steps to clarify the problem, open up the discussion with others, and honestly discuss the situation. If a problem does not exist, clearly document the discussions to ensure that if questions arise in the future there will be evidence the topic was evaluated thoroughly. If a conflict or ethics violation is present, make the correct decision to eliminate the problem.

Managing Founder's Syndrome
or ...
Do you want this organization to continue after you leave?

Constance Carter

Our society is indebted to nonprofit founders, people who felt so strongly about a need or issue that they became passionately and personally committed to creating a new solution. Most of the organizations and institutions we know and love arose from an individual or group of people becoming inspired and taking action to make the world a better place.

And yet, once the organization is established, things can go terribly wrong.

Who is a founder?
A founder is generally the person who had an idea and started an organization. However, the same dynamics also apply to:

> ➤ A group of people, perhaps developing into a board, who started an organization,
> ➤ A single individual or a small group of individuals who bring an already-existing organization through tough times (a growth spurt, a financial collapse, reorganization, etc.),
> ➤ An organization's first Executive Director, and
> ➤ A person who has been the Executive Director in an organization for 10 or more years.

Founder Characteristics
Founders are initiators, creators, and visionary leaders who thrive on building something new, or reviving a previously "lost cause." Founders possess the strong, passionate, and charismatic personality required to identify a community need and create a new organization to address that need. They thrive on making fast decisions, encouraging others to join the cause, and motivating people to action. They usually are high energy people, willing and able to work long hours, sustaining themselves on the

satisfaction that comes from accomplishing their vision. In the for-profit world, they are considered entrepreneurs.

Founders often enjoy being the center of attention and are effective speakers and networkers on behalf of the mission. Often their identity becomes merged with that of the nonprofit organization: the mission and vision actually become who they are. Founders are driven by a compulsion to succeed, and often see themselves as solely responsible for the success of the organization.

What is Founder's Syndrome?
This phrase refers to the founder's resistance to change. Oddly enough, Founder's Syndrome is actually a symptom of success: it usually occurs in organizations that have grown to a point where multiple board members, committees, and staff are needed. In order to maintain the organization's growth, the directors and staff need to be kept engaged and given opportunities to provide input and make decisions. The fulfillment of the mission no longer rests solely with one person (the founder); stewardship of the mission becomes a shared responsibility.

One of main symptoms of Founder's Syndrome is that decisions are not made collectively. Most decisions are simply autocratically made by the founder, because that's how it has always been done. Everyone else merely rubber stamps what the founder suggests. The founder exhibits strong resistance to any change in decision-making, where he/she might lose total control. Boards of these organizations usually don't govern, but instead approve and support what the founder suggests. Planning isn't done collectively, but by the founder; ideas that do not come from the founder usually aren't long-lived.

Regardless of the size of the organization, everyone is relegated to the role of supporting the founder. This dynamic is usually implicit and part of the underlying structure of the organization. When board members say something like, "we go along with whatever (the founder) wants," that is a classic signal that Founder's Syndrome is occurring. ***The board is actually <u>allowing</u> their own disenfranchisement.***

Why Founder's Syndrome Is Dangerous

When Founder's Syndrome surfaces, the problem is usually a founder's misunderstanding of his or her role in an <u>evolving</u> organization. Founders are typically not effective managers and maintainers. That's an entirely different skill set, and one that is equally important. Once the nonprofit organization is up and running successfully, the founder is no longer creating something new; the challenges and thrill of the "chase" are over. The priority becomes sustaining and building, which are usually not tasks the founder is skilled at or enjoys. Due to the growth, different strengths will be needed, such as supervising staff, managing more complex finances and contracts, and building ongoing, sustaining fundraising initiatives. *If this transition is not managed correctly, the nonprofit may struggle or even fold.*

One Founder became the Executive Director of an organization that was in serious financial difficulty. Due to his passion and commitment to the mission, and intense drive and desire for a personal challenge, in collaboration with the board he rebuilt the organization into a strong nonprofit with a capable professional staff. Thriving on these accomplishments, and needing another "fix" of challenge, he went on to triple the organization's size through an intricate public/private funding partnership. However, he lacked the sophisticated management skills the more complex, larger organization required. He also lacked the humility and self-awareness to realize this, and within two years the once-enthusiastic staff began to leave, and the organization's programs and finances were in jeopardy. Ultimately, the nonprofit was sold and the organization's longstanding mission was lost.

A further risk is if something happens to the founder, there may be little or no infrastructure in place, because everything was held closely and handled by the founder. The comment "it's all in my head" may be quaint, but in reality, it puts the nonprofit organization at serious risk.

Finally, being a board, committee, or staff member of these organizations is often boring and stifling. There is no openness to bringing new ideas, no sense of shared ownership or responsibility, and no opportunities for autonomy and creative thinking. This severely limits the organization's potential for growth, adaptability, and ultimately, survival.

Symptoms of Founder's Syndrome
When one or more of the following occur, it's time to seriously consider taking action. (Note: these symptoms may also arise for different reasons in organizations not led by founders. In those instances, it will be important to discern why the problems are occurring and address the root causes.)

➢ The founder monopolizes board meetings with lengthy reports about everything he/she has accomplished; most agenda items are handled by the founder. Board members rarely take ownership of discussions; many may not even participate.

➢ Most board and committee members are recruited by the founder, often without following a recruitment policy. Friends or relatives of the founder are often arbitrarily placed on the board or committee, without input from the Governance Committee, if there is one, which is rare in a founder-led organization.

➢ Standing committees struggle with low membership and lack of purpose/direction.

➢ The founder often complains about being overworked and not having enough time to do everything that needs to be done; he/she resists or refuses to delegate tasks to staff or volunteers. On the rare occasions when tasks are delegated, the founder may be accused of micro-managing.

➢ Staff turnover may be high, as the founder allows few opportunities for staff to take initiative, grow, or be leaders. Board members may also resign when they tire of always being expected to support the founder.

The depth of Founder's Syndrome clearly emerged for one organization that was doing strategic planning. A strategic planning consultant interviewed board members individually prior to the beginning of the planning and learned very quickly that most members felt their purpose was to support the founders and their vision. This fact was diplomatically shared with the group, along with encouragement and opportunities for the board to take active leadership roles in developing the new strategic plan, which they did. In this case, strategic planning brought forth the symptom and provided an opportunity for a solution.

Solutions
Often what keeps founders in place is they worry that the organization they built will fail if they don't stay involved. Conversely, a founder may worry that the nonprofit organization will succeed even more without his/her leadership, making him/her look bad. A founder may have identity issues (*"This job has been my life – what will I do now?"*). Founders need to see that bringing in new people is essential to allow the organization to flourish and grow. One founder had an awakening to this when he was asked point blank: *"Do you want this organization, which you have created, to continue or not?"* Thankfully, he agreed he did, and this acceptance enabled him to embrace making the necessary changes, which then occurred successfully over a period of years.

There may also just be simple resistance to change. Boards may worry about losing the founder's charisma, knowledge, inspiration, relationships, donors, and/or constituents. They may fear losing the founder's institutional knowledge, community reputation, and name recognition.

Strategies for resolving Founder's Syndrome vary widely depending on the situation with the founder (is he/she retiring, backing off voluntarily because he/she wants to do other things, giving up because of changes or upcoming challenges, or is there resistance to leaving?), the composition of the board (are board members prepared to take more active roles once the founder leaves, or do they need training and support?), and the experience and capabilities of the staff (are there middle managers who can grow into leadership roles or do new positions need to be created?). It's important to assess all of these areas carefully when considering a founder transition.

Here are some suggested strategies for successfully addressing and then managing this important transition.

- ➤ Recognize this is a process that will take time.
- ➤ Discuss the founder's transition before, during, and after it occurs, openly and repeatedly at board and staff meetings, to encourage dialogue, creative brainstorming and shared teamwork.
- ➤ Develop a transition plan that includes all of the aspects of the nonprofit organization that will be affected by the founder's leaving. This may include: a communications plan for donors, clients, customers, elected officials, and key community members; obtaining written information from the founder about major donors and key collaborators; and changing signatories on bank accounts, contracts, etc.
- ➤ Develop a post-founder staffing plan for the organization. This will entail creating or updating job descriptions with a focus on the tasks the founder does that will need to be done by others, either staff or volunteers. This may be an opportunity to re-assign tasks differently and more efficiently. Avoid the trap of arbitrarily promoting staff to more demanding positions, unless they are clearly qualified. Most likely the founder hired them, and they may not be the best candidates.
- ➤ Obtaining assistance from a human resources consultant may be helpful at this stage, depending on the complexity of the organization. One nonprofit organization handled these changes by temporarily delegating most of the executive responsibilities to the board chair, a highly experienced, newly-retired corporate executive with years of management experience. The operational responsibilities were assigned to a mid-level staff member who eventually became the new Executive Director.
- ➤ Hire the staff and/or recruit the volunteers who are identified in the new staffing plan.
- ➤ Have the board do a self-assessment to identify strengths and weaknesses. If necessary, provide training for board members concerning how their roles will change post-founder, helping them to build the necessary skills. Board officers may especially need guidance and support as they grow into their leadership positions.

Capacity building grants may be helpful to pay for hiring consultants and training programs to help the board to grow and adapt to the changes over time. (For more on this topic, see the essay "Building Capacity for Efficiency, Effectiveness, and Impact" in Section II.)

➢ Depending on the founder and his/her personality and life situation, the less involved the founder is after the transition, the better. Founders often want to remain on the board or the staff or play an advisory role. These can be successful if the founder truly has knowledge the board or staff need and is willing to stay within the parameters of his/her new role. The danger is that the founder will make it difficult for change to occur and people will slip back into their old behaviors of deferring to the founder. ***In most situations a clean break is best.***

After the Transition

The period immediately following the transition will be a time of re-aligning priorities, growing into new roles, accepting new responsibilities, and opening to new opportunities. Expect that at times the leadership may be confused; *this is a normal part of this process, and it can be managed.* Identifying and addressing the problems and challenges promptly as they arise and before they become problematic will be essential.

It will also be important to periodically step back and evaluate how the process is going. Navigating through this magnitude of change is a big job, requiring patience and persistence.

SECTION II: NONPROFIT OPERATIONS AND EXCELLENCE

"Are we glad to hear that you don't know where you'll get
the money you need. For a minute there we were afraid
you wanted to get it from us."

Artist could not be located.

The Critical Importance of Operating Reserves

Louis J. Beccaria

According to PROPEL NON-PROFITS 2020 an operating reserve is an unrestricted/ undesignated fund balance to help stabilize an organization's finances during times of unplanned shortfalls or emergencies such as a loss of income from one or more funding sources or a large unplanned/ unbudgeted expense.

There are several reasons why having an operating reserve is so important. First, since nonprofit organizations are businesses, albeit ones with a different bottom-line (i.e., mission-based) than those in the for-profit sector (i.e., profit-based), it is incumbent upon them to act like a business in every way. One of these ways is to put money away for a rainy day, as the saying goes.

A nonprofit agency operating with best practices in mind can't rely on someone unexpectedly leaving them a large sum of money to rescue them out of a difficult, unplanned, and un-budgeted financial situation. Likewise, they can't depend on anyone else but themselves to actually establish the operating reserve. Like the old saying goes, "they have to do it the old-fashioned way – they have to earn it."

The following are some suggested strategies for building a reserve fund from the Nonprofit Finance Fund:

Cut Unnecessary Expenses: an organization can engage in zero-based budgeting to review its core services and those that may be lesser-used and, therefore, be a financial drain on the agency. Funds realized from this analysis can be designated to start or add to an operating reserve.

Unexpected Windfall: the board of a nonprofit which has the good fortune to have one-time unexpected funds come its way, such as a bequest or being the one-time chosen beneficiary of a special community event, can decide to use all or part of the unexpected funds to establish an operating reserve fund or add to it if one already exists.

Budget Surplus: instead of continually spending yearly budget surpluses by putting them into expanded services which may not be necessary (i.e., "wants" and not "needs"), the board can add to an existing operating reserve fund or pass a resolution to formally commit to establishing an operating reserve as a matter of best practices and begin securing the organization's financial future.

Operating Budget: placing a small amount of funds each year as a line-item in the agency's annual operating budget for an operating reserve fund contribution.

Capital Budgets: include some funds in the agency's multi-year capital budget designated for the operating reserve; also, such a designation can be made part of a capital campaign fundraising budget.

Planned Giving Campaign: having the agency's board designate a portion of the funds from an organized planned giving campaign toward the operating reserve.

Board Contributions: each year the contributions made by the agency's board to the annual fundraising appeal can be designated toward the operating reserve fund. This is justified by the board's responsibility for financial stewardship. It can be easier to do this than to ask the general community for these dollars since the board should understand the operating reserve need better than the community, which generally prefers its donations to go toward direct services.

Staff Vacancy Savings: funds saved when a staff vacancy occurs for a period of time can be utilized for the operating reserve fund.

Portion of Undesignated Gifts: with board approval, some funds from the annual appeal could be placed in the operating reserve.

The important thread running through these suggestions is that the board and CEO must have the WILL to implement one or more of these initiatives to create a reserve fund or add to it if one already exists in an insufficient size.

Secondly, if the COVID-19 pandemic has taught the nonprofit sector nothing else, it should have taught it that it is critical, as a matter of best practice, to be financially prepared for the unexpected. To be financially prepared, a nonprofit organization needs to have flexibility built into its operations so it can pivot to enable it to continue to offer its services and pay its staff while plans are being made for long-term survival and, hopefully, for thriving. What allows this pivot situation to occur is having an operating reserve fund of at least nine to 12 months in duration. Employing any one of the nine strategies noted above is an excellent way of doing this.

Having a nine-12 month operating reserve fund goes against a long-held and accepted nonprofit sector guideline that nonprofit organizations need operating reserve funds of only three to six months. In today's world, this is not nearly enough. Why?

➢ Nonprofits are businesses and should always be prepared for the unexpected.
➢ If an organization believes its mission is critical, then being financially prepared to continue services during setbacks is the prudent approach.
➢ Clients' services and staff livelihoods, which involve the basics such as food, housing, clothing, and healthcare, depend on the agency's viability.

It is important to note that adopting the nine-12 month target for an operating reserve also needs the buy-in of funders for this to be to be accepted as a new prudent guideline, now and into the future. Here's why. Based on experience at different foundations, we know the psychology of the funding world has traditionally held that the operating reserve guideline of three to six months was adequate for nonprofit agencies. After all, they are only charities!

This rationale has usually rested on the belief that funders don't want their grantees to get too "fat" and complacent and that they, the funders, need to spread their largesse around to groups who may have a greater need than ones with a healthy operating reserve. While there is some validity to this argument, my belief is that this is discounted by a nonprofit's need to pivot and stay in business when external forces create a situation where self-reliance is critical.

It is important for a board to first buy into this concept of having an operating reserve fund and secondly, that the target for the fund should be at least nine-12 months. Once the board has agreed with this concept and the amount of reserve to be targeted, the next step is for the board to officially adopt an operating reserve policy statement.

Essential elements of such a policy statement would be:

➢ Statement of Purpose outlining why the operating reserve is being established.
➢ Statement of what the operating reserve fund should be for, and when and how it can be used.
➢ Statement that this policy is being authorized by the board and signed and dated by the board chairperson.
➢ Statement outlining requirements for monitoring and reporting on its usage.
➢ Statement of how the operating reserve fund is to be invested, if at all.

The wisdom of having such a policy is that it provides a necessary structure and discipline so that the fund doesn't get used up unnecessarily over time. Without such structure and discipline, the funds may not be available when they are needed in the future.

When writing the policy, it is very important that the language be written in such a way to allow for the funds to be accessible and flexible when needed. The dollars are being allocated to help the agency operate smoothly and should not be in an untouchable bank account or invested in long-term securities.

Operating reserve funds are intended to be used for relatively short-term (up to 12 months) temporary financial issues. They should not be used for long-term, more permanent income shortfalls. If this is the case, then the organization has major structural issues occurring. The only exception to this guideline would be if the agency is in such bad shape that it needs to close its doors. In this worse-case scenario, funds could be used for the expenses of shutting down the nonprofit.

The policy also provides confidence for potential and present funders that their philanthropic investment has a measure of stability about it.

If an organization needs to tap into the operating reserve fund for any legitimate reason, it should have a board-approved plan for how to replenish it over some reasonable period of time. This only makes good business sense. If such a plan does not exist, then the purpose of having a reserve fund for the next short-term need is nullified.

In summary, my main message is that it is critically important for every nonprofit organization to have an operating reserve fund for reasons of survival and for leveling out the financial bumps in the road that can sometimes occur in unplanned and unexpected ways. If your organization does not have an operating reserve fund, and it is basically running on fumes and from "paycheck to paycheck," so to speak, then time is of the essence to start one! If your agency has a small operating reserve, it is my hope that you have been influenced enough to restart your journey with the discipline and focused effort to increase its size to cover at least nine-12 months of operating expenses.

Board and CEO Responsibilities: How They Differ

Constance Carter

Picture an hourglass with the board in the top half and the staff in the bottom half. The place where the hourglass narrows is where the two parts of the organization meet. This is where the board (primarily via the chair) communicates with the staff (primarily via the Executive Director). Both sides are connected and are focused on the same overall goal/mission, yet the communication between them is primarily through these two connectors.

The major difference between the board and staff is that the board makes policy, and the staff implements it. The ultimate legal and fiscal responsibility is the board's. Each side needs the other; neither can function without the other's support and input. However, understanding and respecting these differences can often be a struggle.

All too often boards that don't understand this dynamic become totally hands off, in essence saying, "you (staff) understand this, we don't; good luck and we're right behind you." The problem with this scenario is the board is neglecting its support and legal oversight responsibilities. Or the opposite can occur when a board slides into micromanaging the Executive Director, meddling with staff issues, and confusing boundaries, roles, and responsibilities. In this scenario the board is ignoring its legal oversight and policy responsibilities in favor of napkin folding and setting up chairs.

High performing nonprofit boards and staff intentionally create and manage a balance that respects the roles and responsibilities of both sides, forming a strong, diverse team. The following is a sampling of the many issues facing nonprofit management, with the roles of the board and staff delineated. Often either the board or staff will have more responsibility in a particular area. A task may be started by one side (frequently through the board making policy), then the other side takes action, and then the issue may return back where it is completed for a final review.

BOARD RESPONSIBILITIES – In the following examples, the board has the primary authority and responsibility for setting policy, often with input from the staff.

LEGAL MONITORING and RESPONSIBILITY

Although the Executive Director and staff must know and adhere to all laws and regulations applicable to the nonprofit, the final responsibility for compliance belongs to the board. That is why Directors and Officers insurance is so essential for a Board of Directors.

FINANCIAL

This includes oversight of the organization's budget and investments. Staff members work within the confines of the annual budget, which is approved by the board. Other considerations are overseen and determined by the board, such as investments, allocation of grants and gifts, restricted funds, and extraordinary expenditures.

The budgetary process usually takes several months, often beginning with the staff presenting considerations for the next year's budget to the Finance Committee. After discussion within the committee the staff would then make a draft budget. The Finance Committee typically reviews this draft and suggests adjustments until both sides are in agreement. Then the final document is taken to the full board for review and approval. This should be done allowing enough time for any board-suggested changes to be made with the budget being passed well before the beginning of the next fiscal year.

PERSONNEL POLICIES

The Human Resources/Personnel Committee (or full board, if there isn't such a committee) should review all personnel policies at least every 2-3 years to ensure they are updated and current. It is also a good practice to have any changes to these policies reviewed by an employment attorney (hopefully Pro Bono!) if such an attorney is not on the board. The Executive Director should participate in these discussions and be an active participant in all personnel matters. Staff are then responsible for implementation of the policy.

STAFFING

Staffing is dictated by the annual budget. Any additional staffing needs during the year should be taken to the board by the Executive Director for consideration. Specifics about staffing, job descriptions, hiring and firing, and other issues are the responsibility of staff, with the exception of the Executive Director's position, which is managed by the board.

STAFF EVALUATIONS

The board or the Human Resources/Personnel Committee should annually evaluate the Executive Director. The Executive Director is responsible for ensuring all other staff are evaluated at least annually by their direct supervisors. If an employee is a new hire or on probation, there may be other evaluations scheduled. The process and content of the evaluation documents are staff responsibilities. To make these staff evaluations practical and filled with accountability, evaluations should be based upon individual staff goals set at the beginning of the year.

STAFF COMPENSATION

Raises and other staff compensation should be factored into each annual budget. Annual increases for the Executive Director are approved by the board; the Executive Director approves all other staff raises. Salary surveys for management staff positions should be regularly conducted to ensure salaries are equitable. These salary surveys can be done in the form of an informal review of similar positions in like-sized nonprofits in the local geographical or regional area or they can be based upon more formal salary surveys conducted by regional or national nonprofit membership associations. In fact, the IRS 990 form asks whether the board has conducted a recent salary survey to ensure that executive compensation is reasonable.

EMPLOYEE GRIEVANCES

All organizations need to include an employee grievance policy in the personnel manual. Unless the grievance is with the Executive Director, implementation is <u>solely</u> the purview of staff. If the grievance is with the Executive Director, then the Human Resources/Personnel Committee and/or board chair will need to become involved. Organizations also need to have a Whistleblower Policy, which protects an employee or volunteer who has credible information about a legal or ethical violation of the organization's policies. (See Appendix for a sample policy.)

STRATEGIC PLANNING

Once completed, an organization's Strategic Plan should be approved and adopted by the board. The development and monitoring of the plan are joint responsibilities of the board and staff. In fact, it is essential that board and staff work together on creating the plan. Staff have a deep knowledge of the operational side of the organization and its constituents, while the board understands the legal, fiscal, and policy elements. Combined, these areas of expertise complement each other.

FUNDRAISING

Ensuring adequate financial resources is one of the fundamental responsibilities of any nonprofit board. Annual fundraising goals are determined during the budgeting process, and boards that are most effective in fundraising understand that reaching those goals is a team effort with staff. The board's primary responsibility is to be ambassadors and networkers, and to identify and cultivate individuals, organizations, and businesses that might become donors. Because board members are volunteers, their involvement in fundraising is unique and carries a special, very effective message to prospective donors.

VOLUNTEERS

Volunteers (including board members) are subject to the same policies as staff, including training and background checks where applicable. The board is responsible for recruiting and "hiring" volunteers who participate on the board or a board committee, with input from staff. Staff members are responsible for recruiting and "hiring" volunteers to do hands-on work within the organization. Volunteers should have specific job descriptions and be supervised by the appropriate staff or board member overseeing their work.

OPERATIONAL RESPONSIBILITIES -- In the following examples, the staff has the primary responsibility, and the board has little, if any, involvement.

The Executive Director is responsible for all day-to-day operations of the organization. The only caveat is that the board is legally responsible for everything done by and within the organization. Thus, communications between the board chair (and in some cases a board committee) is an absolute necessity to maintain the board's confidence and trust in the Executive Director. Board meetings that include the Executive Director and key staff are the best way for the entire board to understand the operations and issues facing the organization.

BUDGETARY and FINANCIAL

The staff responsibility is to adhere to the budget that has been approved by the board. The Executive Director also must inform the board in a timely way about unexpected expenses or decreases in income not included in the budget. Monthly financial statements should be presented, usually by the Executive Director, to the board so they can monitor the overall finances of the organization.

PURCHASING

Staff are responsible for purchasing, according to the approved budget. During the budget preparation process, staff should provide recommendations about items that should be included. The Executive Director should follow a policy which identifies all purchases (including obtaining bids for work or changes in contracts) and maintains an audit trail.

FUNDRAISING

As noted above, the annual fundraising goal is established during the budget process and is approved by the board. Staff are responsible for developing and implementing an annual fundraising plan designed to meet the goal; this is often done in collaboration with a volunteer Development Committee. Staff are often responsible for the technical aspects of fundraising, including: implementing the annual grants program; drafting appeal letters, proposals, and gift acknowledgments; maintaining donor records; planning and implementing fundraising events; and supporting volunteers in their fundraising activities.

MAINTENANCE

As with purchasing, maintenance expenses should be a budgeted item. The Executive Director should have a monetary limit up to which he/she can spend without board approval. Extraordinary or emergency situations that result in unbudgeted expenses exceeding that limit should be taken to the board chair to determine if the board or a committee should be involved.

STAFF JOB DESCRIPTIONS

Staff job descriptions, assignments, and scheduling should be determined by the Executive Director and the senior staff, with little, if any, input from the board. Long-range work plans, tasks from the strategic plan, and goals should be included.

HIRING and TERMINATING

As noted above, the board is responsible for hiring and terminating the Executive Director. The Executive Director is responsible for hiring and firing all other staff members, often with input from supervisory staff. If a job description requires that a staff member work closely with the board, such as a Development Director, then board input may be solicited by the Executive Director during the search process.

EMPLOYEE and VOLUNTEER EVALUATIONS

As noted above, the board is responsible for evaluating the Executive Director. All other staff evaluations are the purview of the Executive Director. Staff are also responsible for evaluating the work done by volunteers.

DISCIPLINE

The board is responsible for any disciplinary action concerning the Executive Director. Disciplinary action with all other employees is the responsibility of the Executive Director and supervisory staff. The board, often in collaboration with a Human Resources/Personnel Committee, should adopt a disciplinary policy that guides the process. Implementation is a staff responsibility.

The Power of Strategic Planning:
Not Just Something Pretty to Put on the Shelf

Constance Carter

"A strategic board has a view of looking ahead, an insight to look deeper, and competency to look beyond."
Pearl Zhu

Or, as Vince Lombardi said, *"Hope is not a strategy."*

Strategic planning provides organizations excellent opportunities to develop a clear and concise guide for the future, enhance communication among constituencies, and engage new voices in the organization's work. The process provides structured opportunities for thoughtful discussion and reflection among staff, volunteers, and others in the community, which can build consensus, connections, and shared goals. Research shows that nonprofits with written strategic plans are far more likely to report having a unifying vision. Often the team building benefits of the planning process are as valuable as the plan itself.

The 2016 Nonprofit Sector's "Leadership Report" notes that strategic plans are important to a nonprofit's sustainability and effectiveness because nonprofits with a written plan are:

➤ More likely to collaborate with other nonprofits, thereby increasing their funding potential,
➤ More likely to have boards open to taking calculated risks and trying new approaches,
➤ More likely to review the CEO on an annual basis, thereby ensuring quality leadership, and
➤ More likely to have a formal process for measuring volunteer leadership effectiveness.

Despite these and many other benefits provided by strategic planning, some people say it is a waste of time and/or bureaucratic nonsense. Digging a bit deeper, these opinions are usually based on experiences such as, "we created a lovely strategic plan and then it sat on the shelf and no one looked at it," or, "it was an ambitious plan, but we didn't know how to start implementing it, so we never used it."

Those opinions are valid. It takes time and money to create a strategic plan, and to not implement it because it is unwieldy, confusing, or overwhelming is a waste of precious resources, not to mention frustrating and depressing. That is why it is essential that nonprofits develop strategic plans that are reasonable and appropriate for the size and capacity of their organization, and not based on a cookie cutter model that might work for a hospital or university system or a large for-profit corporation.

Seven Tips to Ensure Successful Strategic Planning

1. Choose a planning facilitator who understands the nonprofit organization.

Hire a professional strategic planning consultant who has experience working with organizations similar in size and scope to yours. Be wary of the board member who says "I can do this for you; I do it all the time for my company"; or the consultant who says "I do strategic planning for The Red Cross and Greenpeace – of course I can help you." Make sure the consultant will also create a tactical, detailed work plan for implementing the strategic plan, including specific tasks, person or group responsible for the task, start and due dates for each step, and a budget for accomplishing the task. This tactical work plan will break the multi-year plan into manageable steps that are measurable and attainable vs. a plan that just has impressive, lofty-sounding goals and lacks an implementation strategy.

As one colleague said when confronted with a daunting multi-million-dollar capital campaign, "The way to eat an elephant is bite by bite."

2. Consider gathering community feedback first.

Many organizations choose to gather community feedback before beginning strategic planning, and this can be highly beneficial. Strategic planning is a visionary process: done well, it identifies new ways to grow and new, creative approaches to issues. Asking funders, stakeholders, colleagues, and collaborators for feedback about the organization and advice about what topics should be addressed during strategic planning provides new insights and unique perspectives that will add richness and thoughtfulness to the planning process.

Feedback can be gathered in a variety of ways, including individual confidential interviews, focus groups, large community gatherings, and surveys. Using an independent consultant will facilitate this process, as people are more likely to be honest with someone not affiliated with the nonprofit. The community feedback should be compiled into a report that is provided to the entire strategic planning team and reviewed carefully before planning begins.

3. Build a comprehensive, inclusive, and diverse strategic planning team.

Strategic planning offers an opportunity to bring together diverse voices in new and different ways. Assemble a group including those who will be responsible for implementing the plan to promote investment in the plan's success. All board members and key staff members or managers should participate. In organizations with very limited staff it may be wise to include all staff. Nonprofits that rely heavily on volunteers or have key committee members who are not board members may want to include them as well.

The process of developing the plan offers inspiring ways for different constituencies to work together and learn from each other. One fairly new nonprofit had a board of directors comprising high powered nonprofit and for-profit leaders; the staff were primarily young professionals. The board and staff rarely interacted, and as a result the board believed the staff were "young kids" and the staff were in awe of the board. However, strategic planning leveled the playing field. Working together in large and small groups allowed the board to learn that the staff had significant expertise worthy of respect, and the staff experienced firsthand that the board were human beings who cared deeply about the mission and were, in fact, normal people with senses of humor. The bridges built between these two groups during strategic planning served the organization well.

4. Allocate adequate time and resources.

Schedule enough time for reflection, evaluation, and consideration of new approaches and ideas. Strategic planning is a break in the routine activity that promotes new ways of thinking. It is a time to reflect, review, and take in new information. It is important that sufficient time and funding be provided. Strategic planning expenses usually include consultant fees and facility and food costs for group meetings and large community meetings.

The strategic plan will have impact and influence on an organization's work for several years. The process takes from 2-6 months or more, depending on the size, complexity, and scope of the organization and its mission. For example, a small community-based organization with a $200,000 budget and a small staff and constituency may only need several months to build a plan. Whereas a regional organization with a multi-million-dollar budget, significant staff, and complex programs will require more time. While strategic planning is occurring, it is best to not launch any new initiatives or programs, unless they are previous commitments.

5. Think outside the box, but not too far outside.

Strategic planning stimulates visionary and creative thinking, and promotes consideration of new, sometimes revolutionary ideas. However, it is important that this be done within a framework of adherence to the organization's mission and values and acknowledgment of what is realistic and attainable. An outside consultant can be particularly useful in helping to ensure the plan is firmly grounded in measurable, achievable goals and specific action steps. Lofty, broad-reaching goals that are unrealistic are not going to be useful.

That said, avoid thwarting creative ideas with negativity or an attitude of "we tried that, and it didn't work then, so it won't work now." A program that could not succeed five years ago may be possible now or in the near future, if circumstances and resources have changed.

6. Build an action plan with attainable steps.

Brian Tracy noted in The Gift of Self-Confidence:
"A clear vision, backed by definite plans, gives you a tremendous feeling of confidence and personal power."

Strategic plans are team efforts: staff, board and committee members, and perhaps other volunteers will be responsible for implementing the goals. New committees may need to be formed, staff may grow, and board members and personnel may change. As a result, it is essential that a detailed tactical plan be developed including specific measurable steps of what needs to be done, when, and by whom. Without such a plan, goals can become simply wishes or remain "big picture thinking" because there is no clear pathway to achieve them. A successful plan includes accountability, strategies for managing obstacles and setbacks, and guidance about finding support.

Tom Landry, a professional football player and coach who led his team to 20 winning seasons in a row said,
"Setting a goal is not the main thing. It is deciding how you will go about achieving it and staying with that plan."

The tactical plan is also essential in identifying which strategic plan items will require additional funding or other resources. Because the specific activities are listed, estimating costs and identifying other types of needed support are simplified. This will be useful in developing proposals to funders and potential donors who might be interested in investing in a specific component of the plan.

6. Celebrate and promote the plan's completion

Once completed, it is important to celebrate the new strategic plan. After all, it represents a significant investment of staff and volunteer time, energy, and money. Many organizations provide a special meal for the strategic planning team at the conclusion of the plan; others give small gifts and/or thank you letters.

A new plan provides opportunities to reach out to donors, supporters, collaborators, and the community at large. Press releases to local media, posts on social media, and attaching the Executive Summary to the website are all ways to promote the plan's completion. One organization hosted a special event just to roll out the plan, inviting donors, key community members, and people they wished to cultivate. The event included a review of the plan goals and an invitation for people to become involved. Other options include inserting the Executive Summary of the plan in an e-mail newsletter, noting some of the more creative initiatives, or snail-mailing hard copies of the summary to major donors with personal notes attached.

7. Designate a board member(s) to monitor the plan's implementation.

Strategic plans are like plants – if you don't tend to them, they will fail. The board should designate one or more board members to be responsible for monitoring the board's implementation of their plan tasks, in collaboration with the Executive Director, who is responsible for the staff tasks. If you have developed a detailed tactical plan, this will not be as challenging as it might sound. As board members quickly learn they will be accountable for their tasks, participation increases. Paying attention to the flow of the tactical plan and when items need to be started will keep the jobs achievable and prevent frustration and burnout.

As Adam Alter noted in his book Irresistible:
"If you want to compel people to act, you whittle down overwhelming goals into smaller goals that are concrete and easier to manage. Humans are driven by a sense of progress, and progress is easier to perceive when the finish line is in sight."

Suggestions for successful implementation:

1) Make the strategic plan a standing board meeting agenda item.

2) At each board meeting review which items are due to be done, celebrating accomplishments and asking for accountability

regarding those that have not yet been finished. Extending due dates is always an option, provided there is discussion beforehand.

3) Review which items are due to be started in the next 2-3 months, and who is responsible.

4) Discuss any additional resources, including time, that may be needed to accomplish the task or any changes that may have occurred which might affect the task.

5) The Executive Director reports to the board on the status of action steps assigned to staff.

It is also helpful to annually review the status of the whole strategic plan to acknowledge work that has been done, encourage people to continue, and consider any upcoming tasks that may need to be adjusted because circumstances have changed.

Building Capacity for Efficiency, Effectiveness, and Impact

Louis J. Beccaria

Simply put, capacity-building is the strengthening of an organization's functions so it can be more efficient in the use of its resources, produce more effective results, and be more impactful in pursuing its important mission.

<u>Why does capacity-building matter? Why is it important?</u>

> ➢ It develops best practice competencies/skills for better efficiency and effectiveness.

> ➢ It increases the potential for organizational impact on its community.

> ➢ It promotes a pathway for pursing excellence throughout the organization.

> ➢ It provides a self-assessment tool for collecting information to help determine success in accomplishing the mission and goals.

> ➢ It helps avoid organization instability, promotes sustainability, and makes the organization more competitive in the funding arena.

> ➢ It provides a means for building a strong organizational infrastructure.

> ➢ It can bring an organization to a higher level of operational, programmatic, and financial maturity.

What is a necessary prerequisite for undertaking capacity-building? Simply put, it is the existence of a learning culture in the nonprofit organization. To effectively undertake capacity-building, an organization must want to pursue a vision of excellence in everything it does in the pursuit of its mission. It must desire to get better each day in the various functions that make its machinery work. It must seek to be a student of best practices, learning all that it can in the five major areas of concern outlined below.

It is not nearly good enough to engage in capacity-building because a funder suggests it, requests it, or even demands it. Such an external force will not sustain the necessary motivation required to get better. An organization must have internal motivation.

Capacity-building is a holistic endeavor. It should focus on an organization's problems, issues, or shortcomings, but also its strengths. It sometimes may require undertaking a complete, formal organizational audit to develop a "wellness plan" to improve the agency's overall health. A total organizational audit may require a longer-term investment of resources to determine strengths, weaknesses, and areas where growth is most critically needed in the short-term and the long-term. These resources may come internally from the organization itself and/or externally from an outside capacity-building funder willing to make a philanthropic investment in the organization's mission. If that is what may be needed, then the board of directors, in carrying out its governance role and responsibility, should seriously undertake this journey.

Not all nonprofit organizations are in such poor organizational health that they require an audit of all the functions they perform. Many organizations may be doing just fine in several of the five major functional areas outlined below. In such cases, a major organizational audit would be superfluous. The important message to remember here is that if an organization embraces a learning culture, it must be self-reflective and come to an honest assessment of where improvement is most necessary in the near-term and the long-term.

For example, the self-reflective organization may determine that in the short-term it needs to heighten its capacity for stronger board governance by doing better strategic planning. Longer-term, it may realize that, to compete better in the marketplace of funding, it must strengthen its brand and market itself better.

This last point leads to the question of budgeting for capacity-building. Ideally, it would be great if every nonprofit organization was able to annually allocate capacity-building money in its operating budget. This would establish the learning culture as an important organizational item and, over time, provide the constant fuel for learning along the capacity-building journey.

When we talk about the concept of nonprofit capacity-building, we're referring to something that is for the benefit of <u>both</u> the funder and the recipient of the funder's philanthropy. Capacity-building benefits an organization's funders because it strengthens their philanthropic investment in terms of the organization's efficient use of its resources and its effectiveness in achieving impactful outcomes. Likewise, building capacity helps the organization itself because it develops its strength in a variety of functional areas. It also increases its competitiveness, its attractiveness to potential funders, and its ability to accomplish its mission for the benefit of the community it serves.

Therefore, in order to engage in capacity-building an organization must have the desire to improve its present situation along several dimensions such as those noted below. In short, it must be a learning organization and want to be on a journey toward excellence. In the words of Ralph Marston, a former American professional football player, "Excellence is not a skill, it is an attitude." That pretty much captures what capacity-building is all about for the nonprofit organizations who toil in the vineyard of service delivery if they want to achieve excellence!

Capacity-building falls into five major functional areas; all nonprofits rely on these five capacities in varying degrees.

➢ Mission, Vision, and Strategy
➢ Governance and Leadership
➢ Strategic Relationships
➢ Resource Development and Marketing
➢ Internal Operations and Management

Mission, Vision, and Strategy relate to areas such as organizational assessment and development. This aspect involves an organizational audit where basic questions about the organization's present purpose are examined in-depth. For example, is the mission still needed now and is it relevant to the community served? Is there new-found competition in providing the organization's services in an affordable manner? Will the current business model strategy continue to be effective in the future to accomplish the organization's purpose?

With regard to the organization's vision, capacity-building auditing efforts include such long-term questions as where does the organization want and need to be within the next five to ten years to properly and effectively serve the community? What does it need to do to achieve organizational excellence internally now and down the road? For example, in such areas as governance, management, and service delivery, how will the organization remain strong, efficient, and effective? Is its present organizational structure the right one for the future? Does it need to be streamlined?

Likewise, the organization would look at itself externally to see how it may need to develop and transform to stay meaningful to its host of varied community stakeholders such as funders, volunteers, contractors, and regulators. For example, is the organization's structure efficient enough for philanthropic investments by governmental entities, foundations, and businesses? Can contractors afford to pay for the organization's services? If the organization charges fees to clients, will they be affordable to them in the future?

From a strategy standpoint, part of capacity-building would be strategic planning and goal setting for governance, program, and service delivery areas. Likewise, business planning and goal setting would need to be examined. It would be difficult to examine mission and vision without taking a serious look at how the program (i.e., service delivery) and business side of the nonprofit enterprise (i.e., operations, raising funds, and managing funds) would need to function for success. Program planning and business planning are intertwined.

Governance and Leadership are critical areas for capacity-building. While it is essential to have a solid mission, vision, and strategic direction, nonprofit organizations also need excellent board governance as well as competent executive and staff leadership if it is to be a well-run agency.

One critical area in this regard is building the capacity of the board to govern well. In order to develop and improve in this governance area, the organization must have a learning culture, spearheaded by the chairperson. A board of directors is never so good that it cannot learn new ways to govern better. For example, building the board's capacity to: encourage and establish best practice governance, operational, and service delivery policies; be more effective fundraisers; and be better ambassadors for the agency's services are just several areas among many that could be the focus of building capacity for a board.

Building an organization's ability for succession planning and executive transition are critical areas to cover as well. Having a plan for an unplanned or planned change in executive leadership is extremely important for organizational stability. This plan can be codified by having a policy in place and the proper procedures to follow to activate the plan. While not absolutely necessary, it may be helpful here for the board to engage the services of a seasoned human resources consultant to facilitate the development of the policy and the procedures.

One of the areas often neglected in nonprofit organizational capacity-building is staff development. Sometimes this is overlooked because of funding issues, sometimes because the organization does not embrace a learning culture, and regretfully, sometimes because it just does not occur to anyone that staff development is an important investment.

Let's not forget that executive leadership development and coaching are staff development as well. Staff development is not just for second and third-line employees. It is also necessary and critical for the top executive and senior staff to continually improve upon their leadership skills in the interest of the organization pursuing best practices and a measure of excellence.

Strategic Relationships can take different forms in this capacity-building area. One of these is in the realm of collaboration. In our ever-interconnected world, collaborating with other nonprofit organization service providers has become more important than ever. If for no other reason than funding is so limited and competitive nowadays, working more closely together for service delivery has become almost essential. Aside from reducing competition for public sector and private dollars, collaboration can take the form of promoting greater creativity and innovation for developing new service delivery models while cutting costs among the collaborators. Capacity for client impact can be significantly increased for those served by the collaborating organizations.

Capacity-building can also involve coalition-building. Whereas collaboration is often thought to have a more direct service orientation, coalition-building could be thought of as having a more indirect service or advocacy bent. Thus, a nonprofit organization could build its capacity to be more effective and impactful by joining other groups in undertaking advocacy and learning how to do it efficiently and effectively. An example of advocacy might be better social justice and fairness for constituents in criminal justice reform and much-needed education of legislators on new or improved policies, regulations, or procedures so that the agency's low-income constituents can be better-served with more equity in the affordable housing area.

Among arts and culture nonprofits, a coalition might be developed for a more rational allocation of Federal or State resources to keep the arts and culture community viable and strong. Capacity-building can also be of assistance in helping an organization explore a possible merger with another agency. This could be for reasons such as either organization is not financially viable by itself or that it is recognized by both organizations that the community can no longer afford to support similar, duplicative, and competitive services. Capacity-building here can take the form of a planning grant, for example, for the involved agencies to study the various issues and ramifications involved in merging, acquiring, or being acquired.

Strategic restructuring can be another potential form of capacity-building. Strategic restructuring might be deemed necessary for various reasons, such as: the organization has become too top heavy administratively; community funding can no longer afford to support the organization as it is presently structured in its costly design; the organization must become either larger or smaller depending upon its situation; or a CEO leadership change creates the opportunity to look at the organization in a different manner.

Fund Development is another major functional area that often is and should be the subject of capacity-building. To say that raising funds is an important activity and skill for a nonprofit organization is akin to saying that air is critical for breathing for a human being. There are many different aspects of fund development. The more developed each of them is, the more efficient, effective, and impactful an organization's fundraising can be – not only in the short term but also in the long term. These various elements are:

➢ Donor identification, cultivation, development, and stewardship
➢ Annual Campaigns
➢ Capital Campaigns
➢ Special Events
➢ Major Gift Campaigns
➢ Planned Gift Campaigns
➢ Endowment Campaigns
➢ Earned Income Development
➢ Social Enterprise Feasibility and Development
➢ Marketing, Branding, and Communications.

Building capacity over time in every one of these areas is important. It can and should be a continuing and evolving effort in the pursuit of organizational excellence and short and long-term financial sustainability.

Many of these capacity-building elements are particularly important for small and medium-sized nonprofits as they seek to compete for survival in the ever-more competitive nonprofit sector fundraising environment. It is my belief it is part of a board's governance responsibility to ensure that there is a constant effort to improve in each of these areas as the organization goes through developmental growth and as organizational needs change over time.

Internal Operations and Management Capability comprise the fifth area of importance. Here we are talking about critical areas of operation and management such as:

> - Human Resources
> - Volunteer Management
> - Financial Management
> - Facility Planning and Management
> - Technology Improvements
> - Marketing and Communications of the Organization as a Whole
> - Program Development and Delivery
> - Program Evaluation
> - Risk Management and Business Continuation

Each of these functions is critical in terms of its contribution toward an organization's successful functioning. In order to have a quality, sustainable organization these operational and management areas need constant capacity-development attention.

Collaboration or Merger?

Constance Carter

We've been hearing for years that funders respect and encourage collaborations and are pleased when grantees share resources and expertise. Support for nonprofit mergers is recently gaining increased consideration and interest. In this tight economic world, maximizing efficiencies and avoiding redundancies are essential strategies for nonprofit survival. Collaborations and mergers can be extremely useful tools in accomplishing those goals.

A single nonprofit organization can only communicate with and influence a limited number of people. But when that same nonprofit joins with another entity, their combined networks and community visibility can expand their ability to advance shared goals and individual missions. While collaborations and mergers definitely require time, energy, and effort, the benefits can be extremely positive. They can increase an organization's ability to move an agenda forward, mobilize stakeholders, and reach and influence more people.

Collaborations and Mergers: Similarities and Differences

A collaboration is two or more organizations deciding to work together, often for a defined period of time, to deliver a specific program or project. Collaborations can be formally or informally structured, using a simple memo of understanding or service agreement, or a legal document that clearly defines each party's responsibilities and obligations.

Some collaborations are casual, such as when one organization refers clients to another, or donates supplies. Others are more formal and involve one organization providing a program or service for another, sometimes receiving payment for that service. Some may involve two or more organizations collaborating to provide the program, each one contributing a specific aspect of the initiative, such as staff, facilities, or clientele. Collaborations can last for years or they may have specific start and end dates.

It is vital that all involved parties have a clear understanding of their roles and responsibilities. In a *Psychology Today* article entitled "Collaboration: It's Not What You Think," Debra Mashek explains that collaboration is characterized by organizational commitment, high levels of trust, and a willingness to share. Investing time in building and nurturing those qualities among all parties at the outset of a collaboration is essential for success.

A merger occurs when two organizations combine to become one. They are complex transactions generally requiring extensive thought and negotiations about a variety of issues: finances, leadership, staff, programs, and resources. Usually one organization survives and the other is absorbed or merged into the surviving entity. Sometimes an entirely new organization may be formed.

Mergers take time, often six to eighteen months, and they cost money. Expenses include consultants to help guide the process, lawyers to prepare and file documents, and accountants to review finances and establish the financial systems for the new organization. Sometimes consultants are needed to sort out staffing issues, or help the merged organization change its name, handle branding, and communications.

Five Tips for Successful Collaborations

1. Work with your partners to define success and articulate shared goals. When exploring collaborative potential, take the time to jointly define what success will look like. Each partner in a collaboration should be able to answer, "What role does each member play in this collective effort?" The process of identifying shared goals should also include exploring all the items that may go wrong. Identifying those potential derailments will help the parties develop strategies to avoid them, and jointly develop a shared vision that will motivate everyone to keep moving forward together despite the challenges.

2. Nonprofit partners need to trust each other. In order to share both power and responsibility, the collaborators need to trust each other. Earning trust is a process, but collaborators can seek and intentionally create opportunities to talk about trust issues and identify friction points before they occur.

Nonprofits that already have cultures of accountability and transparency will be comfortable with conversations about trust but others may not be, so be patient, and keep communicating. Some examples include discussing potential challenges, or exploring how the parties will share credit, control, and be open to criticism. One common complaint is "it was a joint collaboration, but one organization claimed all the credit for itself." Or "they were supposed to provide four programs but they only did three. No, I never discussed it with them to find out why; we were too disappointed." Laying the groundwork for handling these situations before the collaboration begins may alleviate problems in the future.

3. Clearly document roles, responsibilities, and expectations. Both parties should determine at the outset whether an **enforceable agreement,** such as a written contract, is needed or if a **mutual set of understandings,** where neither party is legally responsible, would suffice. Problems occur when expectations aren't clearly stated. These need to be clearly written. Plan to put time and energy into doing this; it's well worth it.

Written agreements are useful because they:

- ➢ Ensure that a collaboration can survive environmental or personnel changes.
- ➢ Provide a structure in which the partnership can thrive.
- ➢ Prevent confusion and conflict among collaborating partners.
- ➢ Support accountability by clearly defining roles, responsibilities, expectations, and decision-making processes.
- ➢ Provide opportunities to discuss key issues such as goals, strategies, and procedures during all stages of the collaboration.

4. Issue and Conflict Resolution. Maintain a positive attitude, even if you've had difficulties with previous collaborations. Assume there will be conflict at some point and expect to work through issues when they arise. Most collaborations fail due to not clearly defining and managing expectations and not openly discussing issues when events don't occur as planned.

When things go wrong, discern whether the collaboration's goal is still within reach. If so, move as smoothly as possible beyond the conflict. Acknowledge the issue but focus on keeping the project moving forward together. If tensions or outright conflict are ignored, important signals may be missed that otherwise could lead to improvements and solutions. Even worse, the partnership might be declared a failure without trying to fix it.

5. Evaluate and make changes as needed. When a short-term collaboration is over, evaluate how well it worked. For ongoing collaborations, periodically do a formal evaluation. Gather all partners to review the goals and objectives. Discuss any unanticipated adjustments that were made during the collaboration in response to changes or challenges. How well did those adjustments work? Do we want to continue? Would we do this again? Why or why not? What did we learn?

Again, communication is essential for success – at the beginning, throughout, and at the end.

To Merge or Not to Merge

A merger entered into thoughtfully and with diligence can result in tremendous benefits, increasing both organizations' abilities to expand their service areas, programs, and their internal capacity to create new and better ways to further their mission.

Mergers are complex transactions requiring thoughtful negotiation about a variety of significant issues such as determining the composition of the new board, preservation of programs, financial management, decisions about staffing, and many more. If the organizations are not sufficiently prepared, a merger can result in negative unanticipated consequences such as loss of mission, diminished community confidence, fund raising problems, and loss of future planned gifts, not to mention hurt feelings and negative press.

Three Merger Benefits

1. To better pursue a mission and deliver services more efficiently
When two nonprofits share a common mission and provide similar or overlapping services in the same general geographic area, they face the problems of service duplication and confusion in the eyes of clients and donors. Merging streamlines service delivery, eliminates duplication and waste, and solves any identity confusion.

2. To improve skill sets and grow strategically
When two nonprofits identify they have critical strengths in differing areas (service delivery or fundraising, for example), they may decide to merge. Combining strengths and ceasing to compete for funding can become effective ways to expand services and pursue a stronger future.

3. To improve the financial outlook and improve sustainability
Merging can help a struggling nonprofit achieve improved cash flow and gain access to new capital. A smaller nonprofit with a strong program but unsteady finances may see an advantage in merging with a larger organization that has a solid funding base but does not offer a program comparable to that of the smaller organization. In this case, the smaller nonprofit's excellent program can continue with a better likelihood of survival. In addition, merging can enhance the infrastructure of a nonprofit that has had to cut back on resources such as staff and technology.

In considering the possibility of merging, it is important to talk with key donors, supporters, and other nonprofit collaborators to ask their views about the merger idea. This "merger feasibility study" will help your board to make a more informed decision, and if the results are positive, will give the board and staff a greater comfort level with the merger idea.

12 Steps Toward Merger

1. Pick an appropriate partner. The most successful mergers grow out of previously established collaborations or relationships. It's important that the two organizations have compatible cultures and values and operate in somewhat similar ways.

2. Develop a strong, engaged Merger Leadership Team. The Merger Leadership Team should include key board and staff members from the merging organizations, and a professional consultant. Hiring a consultant with experience in facilitating mergers will speed the process and ensure the leadership team stays on track. The participation of an objective third party throughout merger discussions can also be helpful, especially if negotiations become strained.

This team will create and manage the merger process. It's important that the players be motivated for the merger to succeed and prepared for the work involved. Monthly meetings will be required of this group.

3. Develop a Memorandum of Understanding that outlines the shape the merger will take. Consider questions such as:

- ➢ What will the new organization look like?

- ➢ What will the newly merged nonprofit be named?

- ➢ How are the organizations similar and how are they different? What issues need to be considered in order to blend the parties?

- ➢ What is the benefit to the organizations and the community?

- ➢ How will the newly merged nonprofit be governed: who will be on the board?

- ➢ How will executive leadership be determined?

- ➢ How will financial challenges be met (including the cost to implement the merger)?
- ➢ How will the success of the merger be measured?

4. The Boards of Directors of both nonprofits vote on an "Intent to Merge" which formalizes the merger process and gives the Merger Leadership Team authority to continue.

5. A legal review of both nonprofits is done by attorneys. The purpose of this step is to focus on potential legal issues that might affect the merger process and/or the merger itself. It's important to hire attorneys who are experienced with mergers.

6. Financial audits are done for both organizations. This may be as simple as having a CPA review each organization's audits and IRS 990s to get an overview of fiscal stability, and identify any issues, such as deficits, long-term debt, or endowments that might be important. The CPA may also evaluate the quality of each organization's financial practices to identify any major changes that would need to occur after the merger.

If the legal and financial audits are successful ...

7. The Leadership Team forms Merger Workgroups to facilitate the details of the merger. These groups may work on areas such as: governance, by-laws, staffing, finance, fundraising, communications and public relations, programs, and technology. There may be other issues to address depending on the missions and structures of the merging organizations.

8. The "Plan of Merger" is drafted by an attorney. The content of the plan is determined by the Merger Leadership team. The plan contains items similar to the Memo of Understanding, and others pertaining to how the financial resources will be managed, what will be restricted and unrestricted funds, what happens with assets and liabilities, and how gifts, grants, and endowments will be transferred.

9. Both Boards of Directors review the Plan of Merger and vote whether or not to merge.

10. If approved, the Plan of Merger is submitted to the Secretary of State. Once the merger agreement is approved by the Secretary of State, other government entities, such as the IRS and the Bureau of Charitable Organizations, will also need to be notified.

11. The Merger Workgroups complete their work. This may take several months, depending on the issues involved.

12. Publicize the merger and celebrate! A workgroup may be formed to develop strategies for publicizing the merger, including communications plans for specific constituencies, such as clients/customers, major donors, institutional funders, collaborators, and the greater community.

Lessons Learned from the COVID-19 Pandemic

Constance Carter

"You never want a serious crisis to go to waste"
Rahm Emanuel

After months of pandemic-induced stay-at-home orders, many nonprofit organizations found vulnerability in what they previously thought were well-run organizations. Others were brought to their knees by problems they either did not know existed or were complacent about before it began.

Some of the problems that emerged may not have previously compromised the smooth running of the organization, and thus leaders were unaware of the weaknesses. For others, troublesome situations they had been either trying to manage or were ignoring became significant detriments. Areas of concern include:

1. Technology
2. Boards of Directors
3. Disaster Planning
4. Staff
5. Finance
6. Fundraising

1. Technology
Technology enabled thousands of businesses and employees to continue working effectively and even seamlessly during the pandemic. However, some nonprofits with low-quality, outdated equipment and software quickly found themselves floundering. Staff and board members who lacked computer proficiency became obstacles to problem solving.

Lessons Learned

➤ *Ensure all staff have the ability and knowledge to access the organization's data remotely.* Provide training where needed to be sure staff are current with their computer skills.

➤ *Ensure IT security is robust, and that up to date antivirus and antimalware software are on all computers.* This is especially essential when staff are working remotely. As one computer expert noted, "one bad click and ransomware could destroy an organization's finances."

➤ *Evaluate all computer hardware and software annually to ensure it is up to date and working effectively.* Implement a calendar of replacements and upgrades.

➤ *Provide staff and board training on using an internet-based meeting platform.* Hold at least 2-3 virtual meetings per year to maintain users' skills and comfort levels. This could be particularly useful during the holiday season, summer, or inclement weather.

➤ *Maintain a relationship with an IT company that is experienced working with comparable businesses to provide services throughout the year.*

➤ *Develop a Technology Committee of tech-savvy volunteers to provide consultation, training, and creative problem solving to ensure technology is up to date and that volunteer professional expertise is available.*

➤ *Arrange for professional-grade equipment for employees to use at home.* Laptop computers significantly facilitate the transition from office to home.

➤ *Ensure marketing and development staff are proficient in using videos creatively, understanding e-mail marketing, e-newsletters, and social media.*

2. Board Leadership

The pandemic highlighted the importance of having a knowledgeable board. Many nonprofit boards rose to the challenges and provided exemplary leadership and support of their organization and staff. Others took a hands-off approach, in essence saying, "we don't know what to do, so we'll just stay away. Don't call us and we won't call you." One manager commented, "Board members, just like everyone else, were also handling their own personal challenges during the pandemic, and our nonprofit was probably the last thing on their minds! I had to manage my expectations that they would be available to me as much as I needed them."

During normal times, nonprofits with weak, unengaged, and/or dysfunctional boards can sometimes survive if they have strong, capable staff leadership. The additional stressors and limitations of the pandemic, however, caused such organizations to flounder, sometimes with catastrophic results.

Lessons Learned

> ➢ *During an emergency, institute weekly or bi-weekly virtual board meetings or conversations to keep the board apprised of what is occurring.* These meetings also make it convenient for staff to ask for help and for members to offer their expertise.
> ➢ *Evaluate the board's functioning.* Does the board include the diversity of skills and resources that were needed? What was the board able to do to help? What were they unable to do? What was needed?
> ➢ *The board should regularly review and discuss the Executive Director's job description to help themselves understand the responsibilities.* Many executives commented that the board didn't know what they did, so the board didn't understand how to help.

3. Disaster Planning

Coping with the pandemic and planning for recovery offered opportunities to take out those dusty disaster plans we never thought would be needed and use them. Organizations that had updated and user-friendly plans fared far better than those rushing to create strategies.

Lessons Learned

> ➢ *The board, as part of its governance responsibility, should make sure that the organization has a Business Continuation Plan in place at all times so that the organization is ready to react*

*efficiently and effectively during times of extreme operational
crisis or otherwise abnormal situations.*
- ➤ *Ensure these plans are well-crafted and reviewed at least annually.*

4. Staff

When a crisis occurs a well running team will rise above it, whereas a
disjointed, weak team will flounder. The pandemic dramatically illustrated
the importance of having an effective, cohesive, and supportive staff team.
One staff member noted, "We made a commitment to each other that we
would stay healthy and support one another, and that really worked. In a
small team, everyone is important." Another commented, "At the
beginning of the pandemic we had to fire someone because it was clear
they needed more supervision and attention than we could provide. Staff
had to be responsible enough to successfully work independently."
COVID-19 illuminated any dysfunction that existed.

Lessons Learned

- ➤ *Evaluate how effectively the staff worked together.* Was the flow of
  business fairly smooth or were there slowdowns in particular
  areas? Was this due to certain staff personalities or
  inability/unwillingness to be flexible or perform tasks in a timely
  way? Some staff may adapt better than others to the independent
  work ethic required for successfully working from home. A weak
  link can bring down the entire operation.
- ➤ *Encourage staff members to think and act in new and creative
  ways to promote problem solving and strategic thinking.* The
  ability to respond creatively during a disaster is extremely
  important. One director commented, "For our organization,
  surviving this was all about creative solutions."

5. Finance

Prior to the pandemic, 3-6 months of cash reserves were considered
sufficient for most nonprofits. Lessons learned from the pandemic,
however, indicate that nine months of cash reserves now should be
considered the norm, and a full year's worth is not excessive. Funders
need to realize and accept, as part of their funding philosophy, that in the

perilous and very unpredictable times in which we now live this only makes good business sense. There should be no difference between the for-profit and the nonprofit sectors in how an organization prepares for the future uncertainties. During a disaster, cash flow and financial management weaknesses can quickly become huge problems. (For more information on this topic see the essay "The Critical Importance of Operating Reserves" in Section II.)

> *Reserve funds should be easy to access, such as being held in a regular savings, checking, or money market account.* One organization was caught short-handed because their reserves were invested in the stock market. When those reserves were most needed, the market was sufficiently down to make selling a poor option.
> *Endowment funds provided stability and a sense of security.* Despite the market's changes, endowments gave nonprofits a cushion and reassurance that funds would be available in the future. One nonprofit leader commented: "I'm grateful for our prior supporters and leaders who had the vision to create an endowment; it's how we are surviving today."
> *Monthly giving programs provided some steady income even while other donations were slowing.* Monthly giving options have been steadily gaining in popularity; in 2017 revenues from monthly giving increased by 40%. Research shows that pre-selecting the monthly giving option on the website donation page can increase monthly donations by up to 35%.

6. Fund Raising

The Covid-19 stay-at-home-order required organizations to cancel thousands of in-person fundraising events. Some foundations shifted their giving to nonprofits supplying healthcare and basic needs, creating even more challenges for those in other sectors, such as arts, environment, and education. More than ever, creative approaches became essential. Not surprisingly, organizations with robust fundraising programs and generous, loyal donors, continued to successfully raise money even during the pandemic. Those with weak programs, few major donors, and limited networks suffered significantly.

- ➢ *As noted above, the presence or lack of technology capacity proved significant. Nonprofits with cloud-based, robust donor databases that contained donors' telephone numbers and e-mail addresses could easily connect with donors using a variety of strategies.* Collecting this information year round is a necessity.
- ➢ *Creative, outside-the-box thinking motivated nonprofit staffs and boards to develop alternatives to in-person events.* Virtual fundraising events, videos, and other digital techniques helped to keep donors interested and apprised of the nonprofits' work, thereby encouraging donations.
- ➢ *Relationships with donors became more important than ever.* The pandemic illustrated that many people wanted to and were able to give, and that maintaining those connections was essential. Engaging board members to participate in contacting donors, just to check in and say hello, was an extremely effective strategy for some nonprofits, and helped to keep the board engaged.
- ➢ *Make sure the organization's e-commerce site is functional.*

In conclusion, reflecting on experiences during this pandemic can help to make organizations stronger and more resilient when a disaster of any kind strikes. Adding some of the ideas noted above to the strategic plan will help to ensure that the improvements are made, and that this crisis didn't go to waste.

SECTION III: TIPS FOR GRANTMAKERS AND GRANTSEEKERS

" TODAY WE'RE INTERVIEWING A LONG TIME, WELL KNOWN PHILANTHROPIST... "

Analyzing Grant Requesting Organizations

Part I: Governance Strength

Louis J. Beccaria

Evaluating proposals and the organizations seeking funding is one of the most important components of the grantmaking process, because philanthropic funding is a significant investment in a nonprofit organization. Funders have a fiduciary responsibility to ensure their grant dollars will be spent effectively and judiciously by evaluating the grant-seeking organization to gain a keen understanding of its strengths and weaknesses.

The average well-written proposal will include these standard elements:

- Summary
- Introduction
- History/Background on the Organization
- Statement of the need – the problem the proposal is addressing
- Project Budget
- How the Funding will be Utilized (i.e., Methodology/Approach)
- How the Program will be Evaluated
- Who Will Benefit from the Program
- Various Attachments to the Proposal

But the proposal is only part of the process! What is equally important is for the funder to gain a keen understanding of the strength or weakness of the organization submitting the proposal. After all, philanthropic funding is not just paying for a program or project. It is a long-term investment in the organization and the people and community it serves.

How does a funder assess the organization submitting the proposal to ensure the investment will be a sound one? There is a myriad of ways a funder can do this. One way I have found to be effective is to examine indicators of strength or best practice, i.e. direct gauges, signifying signs, or data that point out strengths or weaknesses of the organization being considered.

Two fundamental indicators of organizational strength are <u>governance</u> and <u>finances</u>. This article explores governance considerations. Part II discusses how to evaluate an organization's finances.

The governance of a nonprofit is considered the bedrock or foundation of the organization. If the foundation of a house is not built of strong material it will be weak and probably not last very long; it may even be dangerous to those who inhabit it. Likewise, if an organization does not have a strong governance structure in place, it too will be weak and lacking in durability and ability to make community impact and fulfill its mission. In fact, it may even be dangerous to itself and the community.

I recommend considering three essential indicators of <u>governance</u> strength when making a funding decision:

1. **Diversity** of the Board of Directors

2. **Activity** of the Board of Directors

3. **Policies** of the nonprofit organization

1. <u>Diversity of the Board of Directors</u>

Nonprofit organizations are given a tax-exemption by the Federal Internal Revenue Service and are therefore obliged to serve their community, whether it be locally, regionally, nationally, or internationally. Their governing board of directors must be representative of that community. The following characteristics should be considered.

a. Number of board members

The board needs to be large enough to include a variety of people representing their community and have sufficient members present to reach a quorum. For the average small to mid-sized nonprofit agency, nine to eleven board members is generally adequate. Larger, more complex organizations will require more members. Effective boards also have an odd number of members to prevent a tie vote on an important issue.

b. Age

Nonprofit governance boards should include people of different age groups to represent a variety of perspectives. This includes the wisdom offered by older members; new, fresh views brought by younger board members; and the different life experiences that people of all ages provide.

c. Gender

Over half of the United States population are women, and they should be adequately represented on the boards of nonprofit organizations. Women and men have different and unique perspectives. These perspectives are essential to enriching board policy discussions and making effective program decisions. To represent any community well, boards should no longer be male dominated as they previously have been.

d. Race/Ethnicity

As a matter of the public interest and social justice, a greater degree of racial and ethnic balance is a strength indicator. It is not always easy to find and cultivate enough people of varied ethnicities to take on time-consuming, voluntary board positions. It is, however, absolutely essential to make it a top priority to do so. Racially diverse board leadership is an important attribute of a strong, high performing nonprofit organization.

e. Professional Backgrounds

The board of directors is the foundation upon which a nonprofit organization operates. Serving on a nonprofit board is important business and has serious personal and organizational implications. It is essential that appropriate expertise be available for discussions and decisions on policy matters, finances, employment, programs, fundraising, and other important matters that arise. The IRS, in granting nonprofit tax-exempt status, requires the organization to be strong and guided by the right professional talent.

Nonprofit organizations need to have a cross-section of professionals on the board representing a wide array of disciplines, such as: legal, finance, human resources, marketing, fundraising, and consumer or community representatives, as well as others.

2. Activity of the Board of Directors
Another strength indicator is a board's level of activity in fulfilling its governance responsibilities. Here are a few suggestions about how to evaluate this.

a.   How often does the board of directors meet?
A generally accepted guideline states a board of directors should meet every other month. Quarterly meetings are probably not enough to provide proper oversight, particularly for small or mid-sized organizations. Larger established organizations with boards of 25-40 members may tend to have quarterly board meetings, but they also usually have very active committees that do the bulk of the work. These active committees often make recommendations to the whole board for ratification.

b.   How many committees does the board have?
Recommended best practice guidelines suggest the following committees be in place:

> ➢ **Executive** (composed of the elected officers of the board).
> ➢ **Governance** (handling board member nomination, orientation, and training duties).
> ➢ **Budget or Finance** (establishing, recommending, and monitoring an organization's budget and financial statements).
> ➢ **Audit** (responsible for hiring an outside, independent auditor, reviewing the yearly audit, and recommending to the board the acceptance or non-acceptance of the audit).
> ➢ **Fundraising** or **Fund Development** (develops fundraising strategies for board approval, special events, grant requests to foundations and businesses, as well as annual fundraising drives).

(For more information on this topic, see "Standing Board Committees" in Section V.)

c. **Other indicators of board activity include:**

> ➤ How many board members donate money to the organization?
> ➤ How many provide in-kind services or goods?
> ➤ How many try to cultivate donor prospects?
> ➤ Does each board member participate in at least one board committee?

Funders like to see that 100% of the board members are donating financially to the organization. This shows commitment and leadership from within. If "family" members who are most familiar with the organization and its work aren't giving, why should outsiders?

3. Policies of the nonprofit organization
The following written governance-related policies should be established to give confidence to stakeholders that the nonprofit is well-organized and on top of its game:

> ➤ **Mission Statement** that clearly states the organization's purpose.
> ➤ **Vision Statement** that envisions where the organization hopes to be in the future as a result of accomplishing its mission.
> ➤ **Conflict of Interest Policy** that is read and signed off on annually by board members.
> ➤ **Whistleblower Policy** that protects an employee or board member if a wrongdoing is legitimately suspected.
> ➤ **Document Retention/Destruction Policy** crafted for the proper historical management of important organizational information.
> ➤ **Business Continuation Policy** adopted by the board and staff in case of some unforeseen disaster.
> ➤ **Employment Policy Manual** developed, distributed to, and signed by all employees.
> ➤ **Strategic Plan** developed and regularly tracked to provide guidance about the direction of the organization and how it spends its time and resources.

Best practice principles recommend that governance-related policies be reviewed, and if needed, updated, at least every three to five years.

A thorough assessment of an organization's governance strength or weakness can be accomplished by asking some very specific questions. The answers will aid the funder in exercising his/her fiduciary responsibility to award funds to the most effective, highest performing nonprofit organizations. (A sample of these questions is contained in the Grant Request Form in the Appendix.)

Analyzing Grant Requesting Organizations

Part II: Fiscal Strength

Louis J. Beccaria

Fiscal strength is the second major indicator of an organization's viability that funders should carefully evaluate.

Funding is an investment in an organization, similar to the way individuals invest in a business to support a product it may produce. While we are attracted to the product, if the business is not solid financially, the research, development, and manufacturing cannot occur. Potential funders are asked to give to the nonprofit organization that is proposing the program or project. At its core, funding is a nonprofit sector business decision. If the nonprofit organization is not fiscally strong, then the program most likely will not be.

In the 30 years of philanthropic work I have done at different foundations of various asset sizes I have found that the following financial and activities ratios are effective indicators of the financial health of a nonprofit organization.

Financial Position Ratios

1. **Current Ratio** measures financial liquidity by dividing current assets by current liabilities. The ratio displays the amount of current assets available to pay off current liabilities. It reveals the short-term financial liquidity, or lack thereof, of the organization. A ratio of greater than 1:1 is preferred and is an indicator of strength.

2. **Investment Ratio** compares investments (or endowment) to total assets. Organizations with investments greater than 25% of total assets can be said to display adequate long-term reserves. Additionally, the greater the endowment, the greater the

investment income will be, thereby increasing an organization's fiscal stability.

3. **Fixed Asset Ratio** measures the proportion of property, plant, and equipment (fixed assets) to the organization's total assets by dividing fixed assets by total assets. This ratio is important because it shows how efficiently an organization is using its fixed assets to create income. Additionally, organizations with fixed assets greater than 50% of their total assets are beginning to display a lower degree of long-term liquidity, as fixed assets cannot usually be sold quickly to create cash. Liquidity is important so an organization can be nimble, flexible, and reactive to opportunities and unplanned challenges that may occur.

4. **Long-Term Debt Ratio** measures the proportion of an organization's long-term debt compared to its total net assets. Although the leverage that long-term debt can provide can be helpful, an organization with debt greater than 50% of its total net assets may begin to experience financial stress because paying off the debt is too costly. This may result in the organization not being able to meet its financial obligations, such as meeting payroll or providing programs, due to the lack of liquid cash. In short, too much long-term debt can shackle an organization and weigh it down.

5. **Unrestricted Net Assets Ratio** measures the proportion of long-term debt to unrestricted net assets. This calculation is similar to the ratio noted above, but it focuses on unrestricted (potentially more liquid) net assets. This is a cash reserve that has grown over time, often called an operating reserve. Its liquidity allows the organization to fund future projects or pay down present obligations.

6. **Net Asset Growth Ratio** measures the growth in net assets from one year to the next. A growth rate equal to or greater than the current Consumer Price Index will ensure that the organization is at least keeping pace with inflation.

Activities Ratios

7. **Overall Source Dependence Ratio** measures the proportion of the largest source of revenue to the organization's total revenue. Organizations increase their financial risk if they are overly dependent upon one source of revenue, particularly if that dependence is greater than 65%. The classic case of this is when a nonprofit organization relies on a single funding source for years, perhaps a Federal or State grant, or a long-time foundation funder or individual donor. If the government grant program ends, the foundation changes guidelines, or the individual dies, the nonprofit can be put at significant risk very quickly. Making up that lost income will probably take time, time which the organization may not have. As in many other aspects of life, diversity here is a virtue. Too much reliance on any one revenue source, no matter how reliable it may seem, can create vulnerability.

8. **Revenue Breadth** measures the diversity of the types of revenue sources that an organization has in relation to its total revenue. In an ideal situation, a nonprofit organization would have revenue from many, but not necessarily all, of the following sources, without significant reliance on any one of them:

   ➢ Public Sector (Federal/State/Local)
   ➢ Corporations/Businesses
   ➢ Organizations (faith-based groups/service organizations/ clubs)
   ➢ Foundations
   ➢ Individuals (annual appeals/major donors/events/planned gifts)
   ➢ Program Fees
   ➢ Contracts
   ➢ Endowment

Organizations with solid financial health typically have a well-diversified balance between earned and contributed income. These ratios provide an organization with a benchmark to be able to compare the efficacy of their fundraising or programs with other organizations of similar size. The amount of investment income should be in line with the presence or absence of an endowment.

9. **Program Expense Ratio** measures the funds allocated to conduct the organization's programs as a percentage of total expenses. A good rule of thumb is a minimum of 75% of funds utilized for programming and the remaining up to 25% used for a combination of fundraising and management. An important factor to consider in these calculations is the method by which the organization allocates expenses between programs and administration. Often these percentages are calculated arbitrarily by an outside accountant completing the audit and/or IRS 990 return. The auditing accountant may not understand nuances regarding how expenses should be allocated, unless informed by the organization. For example, if the Executive Director also provides programs, 100% of his/her salary should not be allocated solely to administration. One often-employed method to accurately determine these allocations is to do a staff time-study for a month or two to analyze how staff members actually spend their time between programs, fundraising, and administrative matters.

   While there is no actual Internal Revenue Service rule on this, this guideline is a good Best Practice to follow. Organizations that allocate a higher percentage of funds for direct service programming usually are more efficient in their resource usage. Those demonstrating a percentage lower than 75% should be questioned concerning their resource-use efficiency.

10. **Compensation Ratio** measures funds spent on staff costs (salaries, benefits, and payroll taxes) divided by the organization's total expenses. The percentage for a well-run nonprofit should be 70% or less.

11. **Operating Reserve Ratio** dictates that every well-run, efficient organization should have some surplus at the end of their fiscal year, ideally five to seven percent. This surplus should be banked

as unrestricted assets to build an operating reserve of approximately nine to twelve months of expenses. The reserve is designed to cover the possibility of a future funding loss or other unplanned financial emergency.

12. **Net Margin Ratio** measures the amount of surplus, or deficit, as a percentage of total revenue. Meaningful surpluses, over time, produce liquid net assets which can build an operating reserve or begin an endowment. Deficits raise red flags for funders and are cause for concern. Asking the nonprofit organization to explain the reason for a deficit and describe steps being taken to remedy the situation will help to ease a funder's apprehension.

13. **Grant Request Proportion** calculates the request as a percentage of the organization's total expenses. Another rule of thumb in efficient grant-making is that no one funder, under normal circumstances, should provide more than 25% of an organization's total budget. (See Overall Source Dependence Ratio and Revenue Breadth above.)

Summary

These financial position and activities ratios provide a guiding framework for anyone responsible for analyzing grant requests. For those of us in the position of exercising fiduciary responsibility with money held in the public trust, I cannot stress enough the importance of undertaking in-depth financial analysis before awarding grants.

However, these ratios should not be used in isolation. When a ratio is out of range, I have found it extremely helpful to contact the nonprofit organization and ask for an explanation of the variance. The answer could be simple, such as a critical fundraising event being poorly attended due to weather, staff changes impacting program revenues, or an auditor being arbitrary in allocating expenses. Providing the nonprofit an opportunity to explain the issue also allows the funder a more in-depth view of the organization's fiscal health and overall management oversight and awareness. This can be essential information when making a funding decision.

The Helpful Information Memo

Louis J. Beccaria and Constance Carter

Few grantmakers embrace the role of mentor while at the same time being an analytical evaluator of grant requests. In our judgment, this is a missed opportunity for the potential grantee as well as the grantmaker. Here's why.

First, sending an Informational Memo to the potential grantee is a way to encourage a positive grantor-grantee relationship while also offering mentoring insights. When the grant request analysis indicates shortcomings or room for growth in the governance and/or fiscal strength of the inquiring agency, we believe this information can and should be shared with the potential grantee.

After all, the funder is supporting the program and the organization as a way of fulfilling both the funder's and the nonprofit's missions. Grants are ultimately made as a financial investment in a nonprofit organization, similar to the investment people make when buying stock in a for-profit company. Investors want to be confident that the company is strong and has the potential to give a good return on investment. Likewise, philanthropic funders desire to invest in an organization it believes is strong or at least has the potential to become strong in a reasonable period of time. In addition, the funder would like the reassurance the organization is high quality and sustainable for the future.

A question might be what good does it do to not give the potential grantee this information, whether they are funded or not? First, because this information can help a nonprofit become stronger and more effective, it seems almost cruel or irresponsible for a funder to not share the analyzed information. Improved governance and capacity can help transform the organization into a better service provider for its clients and a stronger service delivery member for the overall community. There really is no down-side to sharing this information.

Second, sharing the information and tracking it in subsequent progress reports, if the grant is made, helps build accountability for the grantee. This follow up is essential to determine if the nonprofit is utilizing the information that has been offered. Our experience has been that most organizations embrace the information, are grateful for the insight, and respect its importance and validity about ninety percent of the time. We have received written and verbal feedback from numerous nonprofits saying how much they appreciate receiving the Informational Memo. We have also heard the following from more than one executive director: "Now that you, as a funder, has pointed out these things, maybe now my board will listen and implement them. I've been asking them to do this for a long time."

Third, sharing this information educates nonprofit board and staff members about how to improve the overall governance, quality, and sustainability of their organization. It also promotes Best Practices throughout the entire nonprofit community. When this happens, everyone benefits because the universally accepted Best Practices help to promote a healthy nonprofit business culture and greater organizational strength, sustainability, and accountability. For the funder, this information-sharing insures better fiduciary stewardship of the funds that are entrusted in the public interest.

We have included a sample Informational Memo in the Appendix with spaces left for listing areas that need improvement. These areas are derived from the information requested in the Grant Request Form, which is also included in the Appendix and discussed in the articles "Analyzing Grant Requesting Organizations, Parts I and II" in Section III. We believe this form is an extremely important component of a grant proposal as an aid to analyzing Governance and Fiscal strength, two of the best indicators of organizational quality and sustainability.

Below are a few samples of the types of questions asked on the Grant Request Form, why they would be noted in the Informational Memo if the answers are found to be lacking, and how they can be helpful in educating nonprofit staff and board members about Best Practices.

> The question about the percentage of the board members who donate financially, in-kind, and by making fundraising contacts is helpful in motivating the board to become more active. How active a board is can be a critical indicator of organizational strength. Being able to say in the Informational Memo that a funder is interested and concerned about this matter can be very helpful for staff who are trying to impart this message.

> The question about board diversity is similarly helpful in motivating the board to be more strategic and thoughtful regarding board recruitment. The questions help to move people beyond "who do we know" into "what skills and demographics are needed." They also show board members and executive directors the specifics about the level of diversity that a strong board should have.

> The question about standing committees motivates nonprofits to build a strong committee structure if they don't already have one, and to maintain it if it already exists. It educates organizations regarding which committees are considered necessary.

> The question about policies prompts nonprofits to adopt these essential policies, and to review and update them regularly. Since the IRS Form 990 contains questions about these policies, it is especially important that all nonprofits embrace them.

> The question about percentages of funds used for programs, fundraising, and administration can highlight the need for nonprofits whose finances fall outside of the recommended ratios, to educate their auditor about the issue or find a new one who understands the importance of these ratios. Alternatively, they may indicate the need for the organization to change how it utilizes its resources, to develop more efficient and cost-effective fundraising initiatives, and/or to examine its salary and benefit structure to ensure it is consistent with the mission.

> The question about Directors & Officers liability insurance prompts small and emerging organizations that may not know about this essential protection to obtain it. This question can reassure them that the premium for such insurance is money well spent.

Trading Places: Understanding the Other Side

Louis J. Beccaria

Having spent many years exclusively on the grantmaking side of the ledger and decades involved one way or another on the nonprofit agency side, I've developed a sense of the psychology and etiquette about what I call the philanthropic dance and the need for both sides to trade places to better understand each other. Some may call this a kind of cat and mouse game. Whatever one calls it, there are things that both sides need to know, understand, respect, and appreciate about the other. To do this they need to find a way to trade places mentally and walk professionally in the shoes of the person living on the other side of this philanthropic equation.

Considerations for Funders

First, funders need to understand and have empathy for the constant fundraising, evaluative/ outcome, and accountability pressures endured by the agencies they fund. They are trying, in most cases, to the best of their abilities and resources, to do much with little while at the same time having an impact and making a difference in their community.

Secondly, funders need to also understand that they are not the only funder with whom the agency must deal. There are other funders also making their own special requests/demands.

Thirdly, funders should be cognizant of the fact that while they are funding a particular program and agency, and through their largesse hold much influence, they're not the experts in delivering the services they are funding. Thus, funders should not overstep their bounds. For the most part, they should not step out of their funder's role and into the micro-management role of telling grantees how to run their programs or agency. An exception to this maxim would be a situation where complete and total mismanagement of an agency and incompetent governance leadership are occurring. At this point the funder's fiduciary responsibilities come to the fore.

Admittedly, sometimes short of a mismanagement situation, holding back from micro-managing a nonprofit can be difficult and frustrating for a funder simply because things are not being done in the manner which the funder prefers. The funder must hold his or her tongue and step back a bit. Such situations, however, can open up another opportunity to assist through the vehicle of capacity-building. Capacity-building philanthropy offers a good opportunity to retreat from the temptation to micromanage when things don't appear as efficient or as effective as the funder might like. It also allows the funder to project a positive image in offering help without coming across in a pushy or dictatorial way. (For more information on capacity building, see the essay "Building Capacity for Efficiency, Effectiveness, and Impact" in Section II.)

Helping an organization better itself by funding board and staff development, strategic planning, fundraising, or marketing to increase its visibility in the community, for example, are very valuable ways to get a funder's point across about the need for the agency to be more efficient, effective, and impactful. Capacity-building is not butting in; it is being helpful and can be an equally useful philanthropy as making a grant for direct services.

Considerations for Nonprofits

For their part, nonprofit organizations must walk in the shoes of the funder. They need to be aware that giving away money is more difficult than just signing a check and mailing it to the grantee. Grant-making has its own set of pressures. Some of these are:

> Making sure that the foundation's investment portfolio performance is good enough to respond to community needs and meet grantmaking obligations now and into the future,

> Performing sufficient due diligence on potential grantees to ensure that one's fiduciary and stewardship responsibilities as a funder are being carried out properly,

> Providing enough monitoring oversight on grants previously made to ensure that accountability is built into the grantsmanship process and enforced,

➤ Having to say "No" to a worthy request that addresses a critical community need and meets all the funder's criteria because there are not enough dollars to go around, and

➤ Ensuring that funding particular programs and agencies does not promote a duplication of services in the community.

The Grantor/Grantee Relationship

Another aspect of grantors and grantees trading places is their ability to understand the nuances or "etiquette" of their relationship and the psychology of how to navigate it. I have always felt that the grantor should not be regarded as the entity with all the power in the grantor/grantee relationship. There's another element to that relationship many people neglect to consider. This may be a shocking statement to some of our funding colleagues, but I believe it is true.

A grantor and a grantee, by their very nature, are in a symbiotic relationship whereby each needs the other. Therefore, the power in their relationship is distributed between both parties. The power is in the relationship itself.

Yes, the funder has the money to grant, but this money would do no good if there was not a grantee entity to deliver a service that helps the funder meet its own mission of making a difference and being an agent of change. The power in the relationship is the resources that both bring to it – money on the one side and services on the other. In this sense both the grantor and the grantee are equal players. Thus, philanthropists (those who give away their own money) and philanthropoids (those who give away other people's money) should guard against projecting, intentionally or unintentionally, a sense of arrogance, power-playing, or a "better than thou" persona.

Ideally, because they're equal players in this philanthropic game, potential grantees need not act as supplicants "begging" for money to do their job. They have something valuable to bring to the relationship - their services. At the other end of the spectrum, potential grantees should not project a sense of entitlement as that is an abuse of the relationship and can be seen as arrogance.

In a similar manner, projecting a sense of shame or guilt onto the funder if a grant is not made is a surefire way of ruining a new, budding relationship before it even starts or damaging a longstanding one. Likewise, being a crisis monger and taking the position that if the funds are not granted the funder will be the cause of catastrophic happenings is also not a good strategy and another form of abuse of the relationship.

Lastly, there is no need to be an "apple-polisher." Coming forth in a professional, business-like manner solidifies the equal partnership aspect of the relationship. Apple-polishing or "brown-nosing," as it is sometimes called, is just another way of abusing the grantsmanship relationship and should be avoided at all costs.

PHILANTHROPY

Philanthropy rises from noble and generous hearts.

It is a gift that keeps on giving.

It expands the pool of possibilities.

It waves a magic wand and up spring joy and hope.

It always makes the world,

or some small part of it,

a better place.

Though not done for applause,

it gives the givers sharing their treasure

deep satisfaction,

and it puts a permanent and deserved smiley face

on their hearts.

by Sr. Patricia Schnapp

How to Interview with a Potential Funder

Louis J. Beccaria

The ideal way for grant-seekers to explore the feasibility of submitting a proposal is to meet face-to-face with a funder. Sometimes this isn't possible, as some funders prefer the more impersonal approach of having you submit a formal letter of intent or just send them the actual proposal requesting funds. Different funders have different personal styles and philosophies about how to conduct the grant-making process.

However, if a funder is willing to talk with you, strive to arrange an in-person meeting. The uniqueness of your personality, your body language, and your passion for your organization's mission and/or the project for which you need funding all come through more effectively in person than in a letter or the formal proposal. This is also true when your contact with the funder is limited to a telephone call. If that is all you are offered, however, jump at it! This longer distance contact is better than no contact at all.

So, consider the following suggestions prior to and during your in-person meeting:

Preparation

Call for the Interview: As the saying goes, "if you don't ask, you don't get." Funders are not usually going to call you; you need to initiate the engagement with them. Whether you are seeking a face-to-face meeting or a telephone conversation, you will need to schedule this well in advance.

Do Your Research: This is an essential part of interviewing with a funder. It is important that you be aware of the funder's overall grant history in regard to your type of cause, the funder's geographical limitations (if any), the size of its typical grants, any connections between your organization and the funding entity itself or any of its board members, or with the individual funder. A seasoned funder can sense a lack of research right away!

<u>Write Your Script:</u> A personal meeting is often a nerve-racking endeavor, especially for new fund development staffers. Draft an outline of your anticipated conversation to guarantee that you remember to ask important questions you may have or relate a critical aspect of your proposal. Are you seeking funding for a specific project, general operations, a capital campaign project or a capacity-building project? Does the funder provide grant support in your geographic area? How about your cause? Is it a focus for them? Is your potential grant request amount within the range that the funder is capable of granting? These may seem like simple, basic questions but it is good to not leave anything to chance as this conversation may be the only one you will have with the funder. To show these questions written down while conducting your personal interview is not inappropriate; it shows that you are organized and prepared.

<u>Be Ready to Take Notes:</u> The funder may make suggestions about how to strengthen your request, give you names of other funders to call, or offer ideas for a collaborative opportunity with another organization. By taking notes during your conversation you show the funder that you are taking his/her comments seriously and are eager to follow up on any ideas that may have merit.

The Meeting

<u>Begin with a Bit of Small Talk:</u> This sets the stage for a relaxed and congenial atmosphere. Try to establish some commonalities, such as people you both know or common interests or experiences you may share. If relevant, thank the funder for any past support. The trick is to not carry this on too long; 3-4 minutes in most cases is plenty. The funder obviously knows why you are there. So, you need to get to the main point of the conversation fairly quickly. A typical interview will go for 45-60 minutes. Also, I can tell you from personal experience that funders are busy people and you need to show them that you appreciate the time they are giving you and are being respectful of their busy schedule.

<u>State Your Organization's Mission:</u> Clearly describe your organization's purpose, the service(s) your group provides, who the clients are, and the geographical area where the services are provided. If your organization

has been previously funded, these points may not be necessary. However, in those situations it would be a good idea to offer a brief summary of what you have accomplished with the funds that were granted to your organization and the impact it had. Funders love to hear about any actual, concrete impact their largesse has made.

Note the Need: Establish the justification for your funding request by describing the need for the project. Provide data, offer a few anecdotes regarding how individual lives and/or the community in general have been affected by the problem or issue. Also, you can state the observation of an expert or a study on the issue. As for general operations, provide a good explanation of why your organization is needed as an important part of the community's fabric and service delivery network or safety net.

Indicate the Approach Employed: Whether your request is for a specific project, general operating support, a capital need, or capacity-building, give a clear and understandable outline and justification for the approach your organization will take to address the specific problem or issue. Make sure you are clear in explaining this concisely. Rambling explanations of the methodology only hurt your presentation, create boredom, and endanger the grant request itself. Hit the highpoints of the approach to be employed. If the funder feels he/she needs more depth during your conversation, he/she will ask for it.

Discuss Potential Impact: Explain the impact the project will have, with the funder's support, on the problem, the target population, or the general community. Discuss the opportunity this request offers for the funder to be a difference-maker. State measured, practical, concrete anticipated outcomes, not just data on the numbers of people served or programs provided.

Qualitative, anecdotal information can be especially helpful here by bringing the human impact of the organization's services to light. For a discussion on a general operations request, give an overall view of what the organization means to the community and its citizens and how it makes a difference. Qualitative, anecdotal information can be not only helpful but also a very important adjunct to the quantitative information you provide. Qualitative, anecdotal information provides added insight and brings the entire grantmaking enterprise alive, making it more human. While quantitative facts and data are as important as the skeleton structure of a body, qualitative, anecdotal insights could be considered the body's flesh and blood that bring it alive.

Money Talk. When asking for general operating funds, do not be bashful in stating what dollars you really need from the funder to carry on your agency's overall mission. The funder may need to consider a variety of issues: (a) other competing requests; (b) the percentage of the organization's budget the foundation is willing to fund (usually a maximum of 20-25%); and/or (c) the overall amount of funds available in the grant allocation budget for grants.

When asking for project support, state the project's total cost and whether you are asking for support for the entire project or just a portion of it. Remember that a project's total cost entails not only the hard dollars involved, but also the in-kind support it is anticipated to receive as well as the value of any volunteer involvement. The funder may wish to fund only part of the project, perhaps with a matching or challenge component. In other cases, the funder may wish to combine a match or challenge with an outright grant. There can be many factors at work here.

Inquire about a suggested range of dollars that would be reasonable to request. Your research and previous grant history should be able to give you the answer to this question even before you ask it. However, you should ask it anyway. If the funder is even somewhat interested, he/she should be willing to give you some idea of a potential funding amount that would make sense.

If the funder says he/she is not interested in the project, try to discern why. It may be a question of timing, the size of the request, the type of project, lack of available grant funds, or some other factor. This may help you with future requests to this funder or in similar situations with other potential funders.

Similarly, with general operations requests, if you are an organization that is new to the funder your research into the funder's history in making general operating grants should give you a good idea of a reasonable amount to request. If you are a past grantee, be realistic in the amount of increase you are requesting (agencies almost always ask for increases in successive grant requests!). For example, if you were awarded a $10,000 grant two years ago and a $13,000 grant last year for general operations, it would be unrealistic to make a request for $30,000 or $35,000, unless some special condition or circumstance is at work.

Say "Thank You"

You should realize that the funder has given you valuable time out of his/her schedule. In addition, a funder may have also given you some equally valuable free informal technical assistance during your discussion. Enlightened funders will often try to do this to help organizations in a non-monetary manner. Thank the funder sincerely and earnestly before leaving the interview. Within 24 hours of the interview, you should write a personal handwritten note as a more formal thank you so that it can be received within about three days of the interview.

Writing to a Funder: Tips on Strategy and Structure

Louis J. Beccaria

Here are a few things we have learned during our years as grant seekers who are writing proposals and interacting with funders and as grantmakers, meeting with grant seekers and reviewing funding proposals. We pass on these tips to help grant seekers be more successful in their hunt for dollars. These tips are not guaranteed to make your proposals successful every time. However, they will help you to present a professional grant request.

1. Do Your Research Well: This is an extremely important part of your grant writing, even though you have not yet started creating the proposal. It is often said that research is at least fifty percent of writing a good proposal. There are a myriad of resources with information about funders, be they foundations, corporate funders, or individual philanthropists. Such places include GuideStar, 990-PFs, The Foundation Center outlets and publications, websites, and more.

Some of the most basic but very important things to know about funders' priorities are:

- ➢ Geographically, where do they fund?
- ➢ What are their priority fields of interest?
- ➢ Within their priority fields of interest, what specifically are they interested in funding?
- ➢ Do they fund only projects or new initiatives?
- ➢ Do they make grants for general operations?
- ➢ Do they fund capital campaigns? Equipment?
- ➢ Do they fund capacity-building requests?
- ➢ Do they require an initial Letter of Intent before sending in a proposal?
- ➢ Do they accept unsolicited proposals?
- ➢ Do they make matching or challenge grants?
- ➢ Do they engage in Program-Related Investments (also called PRIs)

If possible, try to supplement your research with a personal interview or at least a telephone call where you can speak in a more informal manner with the funder. You may uncover some subtleties about the funder's practices. (For more information on this topic see the essay "How to Interview with a Funder" in Section III.)

2. Develop a Reader-Friendly Text: Grant seekers should write in well-crafted, simple declarative sentences. The paragraphs should be relatively short, inviting the readers to make their way through the text logically and effortlessly. Short paragraphs make for more white space, whether on paper or on a screen, and this creates an invitation for proposal readers to read more because the text appears less imposing.

3. Use Language to Your Own Advantage: We recommend that when appealing for money, go for both the funder's head and heart at the same time. Grant-seekers should support their ask with facts and figures that demonstrate they know what they are talking about and have researched the matter sufficiently to make this appeal. Likewise, they also must dramatize their proposal enough so that the person reading it feels urged to take action. The grant-making reader should want to read further and grasp the urgency of the appeal and the opportunity to make a difference. Simply appealing to the brain may be satisfying to the usually well-educated reader who may find the text interesting intellectually. However, this may not necessarily move the person to action with a sense of urgency to fund the request.

When a grant-writer brings the heart into the appeal, the reader engages on a different level that activates another part of the brain: that which draws out feeling, empathy, and compassion. An example of this might be: "The abuse of thousands of children in the United States each year not only robs them of their childhoods but has long-lasting impacts on their ability to be healthy, productive, well-adjusted citizens as adults."

4. Refer to Notable Sources: It can be very helpful to use a quotation or two from notable sources to establish the credibility of the case you are making. Facts, figures, and charts are nice and helpful but never underestimate the value of calling upon the testimony of a recognized

expert or study that helps to educate the funder about the issues being addressed.

It's a fact that most funders are often not experts in any particular field. They are frequently generalists who have a breadth of knowledge in several areas but often do not have in-depth knowledge about specific issues. So, they would naturally value experts as they evaluate what they're reading and consider its urgency.

5. Being Word-Efficient Is a Good Thing: In simple language, never use six words when two words will do. Grant seekers are not getting paid by the number of words they write, and the readers of their proposals are not getting paid by the number of words they read. Be stylistically economical. I know from experience that funders are almost always very busy people. They appreciate proposals that get to the point.

In fact, it can be to a grant-seeker's detriment to write a tome. Long-winded, verbose proposals can confuse the issues and be interpreted as being written by someone who doesn't know what they're talking about. There is no need to impress a potential funder with long, multi-syllable words. Correct English is essential, but big words are not.

6. Don't Exaggerate: One sure way to sink a proposal is to exaggerate and employ subjective assertions. If what a grant-seeker is "selling" in the proposal is a legitimate problem or need in the community, then the mere statement of the real facts and situations as they stand will be sufficient to make the case.

Don't compromise the proposal's content. While being generalists in most instances, funders are not unintelligent people. Quite the contrary. Being intelligent, and in many cases also experienced grant makers, they can see through exaggerations and subjective assertions very easily.

7. Speak to the Correct Audience: Be sure that the language used in the proposal's text speaks to the audience to be reached. An example of this is if a grant seeker is writing to a foundation or a business philanthropy that has a scientifically related mission, such as medicine or engineering.

It would not be smart to use more subjective and artistically oriented or flowery language that might be employed when writing to a funder who concentrates on the arts or education.

Similarly, in the case of writing to a family or independent, community-oriented foundation, which most likely is not staffed or governed by experts in any one field, make sure that the language used is not the language of the "insiders" in a field. In most cases, the proposal will be read by people who are generalists. They need to understand what is being written if they're going to fund your proposal.

8. Avoid Using Jargon and Undefined Acronyms: All professions have their own way of expressing themselves, and they often use jargon familiar only to those in that profession. As noted above, grant seekers should keep in mind that most of the people who will be reading their proposals are generalists with liberal education backgrounds who may have only a surface knowledge of the field addressed in a given proposal. So, grant seekers should know that when they use jargon, they do so at their own peril. Such language can be counterproductive. A proposal needs to build a bridge between the issue the proposal is addressing and the funder. Using jargon that the funder cannot understand may irritate them and can destroy the bridge.

Likewise, be cautious about the use of acronyms. If an acronym must be used to avoid redundancy or to simplify the writing, be sure to define it when it is first used in simple, easy to understand language.

9. Don't Shoot for the Moon: Always request an amount within the funder's typical range of grants. The research done prior to writing a grant request will help you determine an appropriate amount.

If your research shows that a foundation has generally given the bulk of its grants in the range of $10,000 to $20,000 but one or two of them have been granted in the $75,000 to $100,000 range, there is probably a good likelihood that there is a special reason for this difference. Either a very special case has been presented to them (an emergency or otherwise unique situation that needed to be addressed) or the group that was funded had an "in" somehow with the foundation's trustees and an exception was made. Yes, philanthropy is not a perfect world and relationships DO matter.

10. Generic Proposals are a No-No: Always customize a proposal or a letter of request to a funder. Make every attempt to contact the funder, either in person or at least by telephone, to discuss the request before the keys on your computer are touched. This not only can save considerable time for you, the grant writer, but also for the funder. If the grant seeker makes a request that is clearly outside the funder's mission, grant submission schedule, or geographical interest area, this will waste the funder's time and show at least two things: you didn't do your research well enough, and you are an unsophisticated and inexperienced grant writer. This type of behavior can seriously affect the success rate of the proposals you write.

A case in point: I know of a foundation colleague who was the director of philanthropy for the large, well-known computer company named IBM. She told me she had recently received a very well-written proposal; in fact, she said that it was one of the best that she had seen in all her years of reading proposals. There was only one major problem with it, she said. The organization was asking for the donation of ten computers from DELL, a competing computer company. Needless to say, that proposal was not funded!

11. Have Someone Else Read Your Proposal Before Sending It Out: It is always a good idea to have the proposal read by one or two people who have not been involved in writing it. It's amazing how they will be able to pick out inconsistencies, confusing language, and mistakes when the grant writer can't. If the above-noted organization that was asking for DELL computers from the IBM Corporation had taken this simple step, they would not have encountered the embarrassing situation that they did. They just may have gotten those ten computers they requested.

Andrew Carnegie had a company that forged steel
And sold it for many billions of dollars…How unreal.
His was richer than Rockefeller and Croesus combined
Yet, hoarding it all did not come to mind.
Instead he decided to invest in charities
Building in the US more than 3,000 libraries.
And, now, thanks to him, America can books freely read
Because rich, but generous Andrew
Refused to succumb to greed.

© 2020 June J. McInerney

"LORD, I'D LIKE TO OBEY YOU—REALLY I WOULD, HOWEVER..."

(when you don't want to do something, you can always find a reason not to.)

Recruiting Board Members: The Right Questions To Ask

Louis J. Beccaria

What are the questions that should be asked when interviewing prospective board members? What should you ask to recruit the best possible person to help guide the organization at that particular time? What clues do you need to look for in a social-emotional intelligence sense? Here are eight questions I recommend you ask.

1. Are you aware of the legal and financial responsibilities of a board member?

Very often people who desire to serve on a nonprofit board of directors have little or no understanding of what the job entails, and therefore do not consider that having a seat on a board brings with it both legal and financial responsibilities. In fairness to both the organization and to the board candidate, this needs to be discussed during the recruiting process.

Briefly put, legal responsibility lies in three areas: Duty of Care, Duty of Loyalty, and Duty of Obedience. **Duty of Care** means that board members are responsible for attending the vast majority of board meetings, being properly informed on important agency issues and programs, and being up-to-speed on reports that are provided by staff. In the realm of **Duty of Loyalty**, candidates should know that when they join the board, they must avoid any actual or perceived conflicts of interest. They must put aside their own personal or professional interests and place the organization's affairs as their number one priority. Lastly, **Duty of Obedience** means that board members are responsible for remaining faithful to the organization's vision and mission, as well as making sure that the organization adheres to applicable Federal, State, and Local laws, rules, and regulations.

Board member financial responsibility revolves around the concept of accountability. Board candidates need to be aware that, as board members, they have the overall fiduciary duty for the administration, investment, monitoring, and use of the organization's assets as well as care for the long-term financial stability of the organization. As a group, board members also must ensure that adequate controls are in place to protect the agency from serious financial errors and fraud. It is important, in my view, that board candidates be made aware of these legal and financial responsibilities so they can make an informed decision about joining the board.

2. What "gifts" can you bring to our organization?
You're not interviewing someone to join a book club or a monthly breakfast or lunch get-together. You're interviewing for a serious business need because your nonprofit organization IS a business. It's a business whose bottom line is its mission which is very important to the community it serves. This board governance position has legal, financial, and fundraising responsibilities. Likewise, you are asking potential candidates to join the board for special reasons. You're offering them an opportunity to make a difference in the community. Candidates, in-turn, need to offer some "gift" to complete the transaction. Joining a board is a two-way proposition. There are no doubts about it.

The goal is to recruit someone who has something tangible to bring to the table. Does the candidate add to a demographic that the organization needs represented on the board? Does he/she help the organization's governance to be more reflective of the community it serves, i.e., age, gender, race, or ethnic background? Does the person potentially provide a professional skill and expertise that you need to enhance the board's governance quality? Does the person bring community contacts and influence needed by the board? Can this person play a fundraising role (and there are several) to help the organization sustain itself?

3. Why do you want to join our board of directors?
This is a critical question to ask. You want to make sure that the person is interested in joining the board for the right reasons. Does the candidate have the time to commit to the organization's schedule of board and committee meetings? Does the person have the energy and interest to take on whatever specific assignments that may arise related to their professional expertise? Is he/she willing and able to serve, as best practice recommends, on a least one board committee?

In the course of the interview process it is very important to try to pick out "red flags" regarding people who seem to express a true interest in being on your board but for the wrong reasons. Is the person just interested in padding his/her resume so that association with your organization can help him/her move up the corporate ladder? Will the candidate's personality fit with the board's governance culture? Does the person demonstrate a less than collegial manner? Does the candidate seem to be too autocratic? Is there a personal agenda of some type that could impede the pursuit of the organization's mission? Does the person have a sense of humor (very important in any group activity!). All of these are critical questions to ask.

4. Can you be an ambassador for our organization?

One of the essential roles for any board member is to be an ambassador. Webster's Dictionary defines "ambassador" as "a helper, an agent, a messenger, or a special representative." In the nonprofit world, a member of an organization's board of directors is all of these. While it is not strictly a matter of governance, a board member's ambassadorial role is essential in both a public and a community relations sense.

While this ambassadorial role is so essential and one of the easiest to play, some people may not be comfortable playing it. This hesitance should be discerned during the recruitment process. Some people see themselves as strictly behind-the-scenes people. Effective board members need to use every opportunity to spread the word about the organization they represent. Helping the organization gain better community recognition by spreading the word about its mission and why it's important in the community is a most valued and needed role. In this sense a board member is a very special volunteer representative whose words and actions carry a lot of weight in the community.

5. Do you have a passion for the cause?

My philosophy is that effective nonprofit agency board members need to feel a sense of passion for the agency's cause. They need to feel that "fire in the belly" that gives them the energy to spend the volunteer hours it takes to govern well. If a board member does not have this passion, then they can quickly become bored or ineffective, and basically just take up a board seat that someone who does have this passion could be occupying.

So, when recruiting a potential board member, you might ask: What motivates you to want to be a board member? Is there a personal connection to our cause and mission, either in your present or your past life, that makes you feel this is the right place to spend your volunteer time? How does our mission make you feel that you can make a difference?

6. What do you feel are the characteristics and qualities of an outstanding board member?
This question will make the potential board member think. It should reveal a bit about how reflective he or she is. This question is not meant to be a test. It's intended to see what the person's outlook and perceptions are about leadership. You hope that the person will answer with some ideas that typically are associated with outstanding leadership: vision; dedication; passion for the cause; a strategic thinking; organization; consistent follow-through on commitments. You're not interested in the person's thoughts about the qualities of just any board member, but an outstanding one. There's a big difference.

7. Do you feel comfortable in participating in fundraising at some level?
Some people practically break out in hives when the word "fundraising" is brought up. In today's nonprofit world, it's considered part of the board's governance responsibility to provide fundraising leadership. This leadership role can be carried out in several different ways. One is to make a personal donation to the organization that is consistent with that person's economic means. Another is to help get funds through sharing their network of community and work-life contacts. Still another is to provide creative ideas on where to look for and how to generate dollars. Ideas on a new corporate or foundation connection that could be made or a new special event come to mind here. Being a connector to potential funding resources can be almost as important as actually giving money itself.

8. What kind of autonomy does the person have over his/her calendar?
Some other relevant questions to ask might be: Do you have a reasonably flexible work schedule? Do you travel a lot for your job? Can you make occasional daytime meetings? Do you have personal family responsibilities that might hinder your being an active board member? Are

you willing to give up a portion of the personal free time you now have in your life to attend board and committee meetings as well as fundraising events sponsored by the agency?

In order to be a good board member, at a minimum, board members need to be available and attend meetings if their outstanding leadership qualities are to be demonstrated.

<u>In Summary</u>
The single biggest problem with interviewing potential board member candidates is that they often are not really interviews at all! When invited to lunch, for example, to discuss a potential board position, candidates sometimes come to the interview assuming this volunteer job is already theirs if they want it. The person or committee doing the interviewing sells and persuades, but typically does not vet the candidate in any substantive way. Real discussions about the "dreaded" fundraising obligation are often swept under the rug for fear of chasing the prospect away.

Vetting potential candidates for a seat on the organization's board should be a thorough and thoughtful process. When the person's name is put forth, it is important to do a bit of background checking and get informal references from current board members or others in the community. After all, that person will be representing the organization. Internally, there is the need to understand the person's personality, the "gifts" that they can bring to the organization's governance, and to see if they will fit in with the culture of the agency. Lastly, and equally important, is the fact that if you are recruiting board members for an organization that serves children and youth, you must do background checks on all candidates. It's the law!

(For more information on this topic, see "Questions to Ask about Joining a Board" in the Appendix.)

Board Member Term Limits

Louis J. Beccaria

I am an unabashed opponent of volunteers spending the rest of their lives serving on one nonprofit board. Call me "old school" but so be it. The following is a litany of reasons why I believe nonprofit organizations should establish and enforce term limits as a matter of good practice.

I believe there are strong disadvantages of board service without term limits, and this belief goes not only for nonprofit organizations but also for foundations, corporations, or any other group that has a mission to accomplish something of importance.

My rationale for my position on this issue is as follows:

Term limits create a natural avenue for bringing new people with new ideas, experiences, and professional perspectives, as well as varied backgrounds to the endeavor. For any organization to grow and prosper in the long-term, this is essential.

Limiting board terms is a good way of getting the "dead wood" off the board. To keep ineffective people on a board indefinitely is tantamount to demonstrating leadership weakness and is a prescription for stagnation in the pursuit of a group's mission. Often those who stay too long begin to lack personal and organizational challenge for the work at hand. They may utter such words as: "We've always done it this way!" Likewise, they may begin to have erratic attendance, in effect, saying by their absence "I've heard all this before." Such an attitude is the beginning of the death march for any organization.

No board member owns the organization. Board service without limits can create an atmosphere of ownership by long-serving members. Nonprofit organizations belong to the community, and there should be ample opportunity for a diverse array of community members to serve the group's mission and contribute their time and talents to the enterprise. Board service is not meant to be a cushy club for a chosen few. If a particular board member's presence, influence, and input are so critical, then the organization should strongly consider establishing an advisory board/committee so that the organization can provide a valued place for such individuals. This arrangement would allow these people to maintain their close affiliation with the nonprofit and continue making a contribution.

Having term limits creates the opportunity to bring more and different leadership styles to an organization's governance process. At different times in a nonprofit's lifecycle, a variety of leadership approaches is needed, advisable, and often required. The **birth phase** of a nonprofit agency, for example, requires much volunteer energy, resourcefulness, and, one could say, an entrepreneurial spirit. The **growth or adolescent period** may demand board members with expertise and interest in such areas as marketing, strategic planning, and fundraising to get the agency to the maturity phase. Still, during the **maturity phase** of the lifecycle, board members with totally different styles, ideas, and experiences will be needed. Some examples might be expertise in program evaluation, investment performance, and risk-management. Turning board seats over periodically (e.g., every three or four years in a staggered pattern is considered a matter of best practice) promotes a situation that ensures that new energy is brought to the organization's overall governance in such areas as policymaking, human resources, finance, and fundraising.

Defined terms create the capability to have both "new blood" and "seasoned people" on the board at the same time, creating a rich mixture of the old and the new. This is where institutional memory meets with a fresh look at why and how things are done. Term limits naturally create a situation that has a beginning and an end. There is a defined time period to make one's mark, so to speak. With term limits there is much less likelihood that people will "retire on the job."

Not only do term limits allow institutional memory to be garnered by the mixing of the old and the new, but they give a chance for constituencies to be represented who have previously not had a voice. As communities change and their demographic mix gets altered, so should the board representation. It is a well-known maxim in the nonprofit world that public charity agencies should mirror, as much as possible, the area's racial, ethnic, economic, age, gender, and professional make-up. Board seats occupied for too long by the same volunteers over an extended time-period fly in the face of this maxim.

And, most importantly, with term limits, the "old boys/old girls club" atmosphere never gets a strangle-hold on a board. When this "club" takes over, boards tend to get lax in their governance responsibility and vigilance over the organization's management, i.e., its programming, finances, fundraising, and policymaking. Without proper vigilance and monitoring, there also is a tendency for the board to let the group's senior management (the President, CEO, or Executive Director) assume more power than is healthy. The balance of power between board and the agency staff leadership can become compromised.

Keeping Board Members Inspired

Louis J. Beccaria

Attracting and recruiting good board members is the keystone for developing strong, effective, and impactful organizations. But what happens once these board members, who are well-qualified, motivated, and ready to give their valuable time and expertise, come on board? Too often the time and effort that has gone into the board member recruitment process is not followed-up with keeping these volunteers inspired. It is difficult for good board members to be effective and to make a difference if they are not inspired and given reasons to be motivated. Maybe you have experienced this situation yourself.

Here are six tips for keeping board members inspired based upon my own nonprofit board experiences – both good and bad.

1. Provide a Good Board Orientation for New Board Members
In many cases new board members are not only new to the organization's board of directors but they are also new to the nonprofit sector. This is particularly true if they happen to be coming from the for-profit corporate world which is generally different in its culture, bottom line mission, and available resources to accomplish its goals.

However, whatever the new board members' backgrounds may be - corporate businessperson, retired senior citizen from the local community, consumer of the organization's services, nonprofit professional, teacher, doctor, accountant, etc., it is important to remember that they are new to your organization and its particular history, culture, mission, services, and challenges. Therefore, they need to become acclimated to these issues to get off on the right foot, so to speak. There is nothing so bewildering as a board member looking like a deer in the headlights because they lack a good orientation about what they have just committed themselves to do.

First, as matter of best practice, there should be a Board Orientation Manual developed by the organization's Governance Committee (see the Appendix for a sample manual table of contents). This manual should be given to new board members to keep for future reference. In addition, the contents of this Board Orientation Manual also should be discussed in a comprehensive and informative Board Orientation Session lasting several hours. Suggested items to include are:

➢ *History of the Organization*
➢ *Organization's Mission Statement*
➢ *Organization's Vision Statement*
➢ *Organization's By-Laws*
➢ *IRS 501(c)(3) Tax-Exemption Statement*
➢ *Organization's Current Operating & Capital Budgets*
➢ *Latest Annual Report*
➢ *Latest Independent Audit & IRS 990 Form*
➢ *List of Fellow Board Members and Their Contact Information*
➢ *Board Member Position Description*
➢ *Listing of Board Members' Legal & Financial Responsibilities*
➢ *List of Current Board Members' Terms*
➢ *List of Board Committees & Their Charters*
➢ *Several Recent Board Meeting Minutes*
➢ *Board & Committee Meeting Calendar for the Year*
➢ *List of Best Practice Polices Currently in Place:*
  *Strategic Plan
  *Conflict of Interest Statement
  *Annual Conflict of Interest Disclosure Statement to be Signed
  *Whistle-Blower Policy
  *Document Retention and Destruction Policy
  *Business Continuation Plan
  *Employee Human Resources Handbook
  *Executive Director Compensation Policy
  *Nondiscrimination Policy

2. Present an Organized Image

As human beings it is natural for us to desire a sense of structure and organization in whatever activities we choose to engage ourselves. There are several reasons why:

➢ It eliminates confusion

- ➤ It helps to make us feel more productive
- ➤ It enhances the opportunity to feel good about ourselves as board members
- ➤ It gives guidance for present and future board activities
- ➤ It guards against wasting time at board meetings

The good chairperson of a nonprofit organization, as the agency's governance leader, needs to be cognizant of these issues. It is important for the chairperson to employ the following to promote the image and reality of being organized:

- ➤ It guards against wasting time at board meetings. Have regularly scheduled meetings dates so board members can know ahead of time and set their personal calendars.
- ➤ When recruiting board members, make sure they know why they are being recruited and what special talent/expertise they are expected to employ to help the organization achieve its mission.
- ➤ Make sure that each board member participates on at least one board committee.
- ➤ Ensure that each board committee has a charter to guide its activities.
- ➤ Stress that each committee have annual goals to be accomplished for accountability purposes.
- ➤ Avoid rambling board meeting discussions characterized by a lack of focus; do not allow the meetings to be regularly dominated by ego-tripping board members.
- ➤ Promote a board culture and atmosphere of openness, free-thinking, acceptance, mutual respect, and learning to appeal to the rational side of board members.

3. Assign Board and Committee Tasks That Board Members Can Enjoy

No doubt you have heard the saying of "putting a square peg in a round hole." There is nothing less inspiring to a board member than being assigned to a task that he or she either has no interest in or is unable or unprepared to do. The result is often a lack of productivity, lack of motivation, and diminished inspiration on the part of the board member. It is a quick way of turning a potential long-term, productive volunteer into a very short-term unproductive one! For example, it would be fruitless for a board chairperson to assign a board member with a real estate background and no fundraising experience or interest to the fund development committee.

Board members are volunteers who are offering their valuable time and expertise free of charge. They should be handled with more respect than being directed to do something that is outside of their comfort zone. It is important to provide potential board members a choice of committees and/or tasks that coincide with their interests and motivation.

Likewise, people often like to collaborate by working in teams. Having two or three board members work together on a task for which they are properly suited and motivated is always a winning approach. They get to share ideas, learn from each other, help each other out, and demonstrate their creativity in coming up with solutions to the task at hand. Motivated people working together can almost always create a situation in which the end result is greater than the sum of its parts!

4. Provide Positive Feedback

One former mentor, who was very influential, had a wonderful saying for leadership: "You can always accomplish more with honey than with vinegar!" These words apply to this point on positive feedback. It costs nothing to say positive things to keep a board member inspired -- whether the things accomplished have been small or large, easy or difficult.

It is part of human nature to want to hear positive things said to us when we have accomplished something. There are two schools of thought on this, however, that I have identified. One school of thought, believes that such positive feedback is unnecessary and takes the approach of "well, that is what they were supposed to do in the first place so why give positive feedback? They were only doing what was expected of them." The other school of thought takes the opposite stance. Leaders who employ this latter approach believe in inspiring people for even the little things they do. These leaders are more attuned to the social-emotional intelligence aspect of human beings. They believe that they can instill greater satisfaction in their board members' contributions and provide inspiration by the "honey approach" rather than the "vinegar approach."

5. Give Them Something To Do
Right from the get-go, give new and veteran board members some tangible, concrete, practical tasks to accomplish. This could be in the form of a special Ad Hoc organizational problem or issue needing to be addressed that relates to their interest and capability. If this is the case, it is important to provide them with the necessary moral support and resources to ensure possible success if they are to stay inspired.

Another approach is to make sure that the board committee(s) they join has goals that relate to its charter, a timeline for completion, and accountability in the form of regularly reporting to the board.

6. Instill a Board Learning Environment
Assuming that an organization has recruited people who are motivated by the mission and vision, and who are interested in achieving a sense of excellence in everything the agency does, then board members should enjoy being a part of a group environment that promotes learning and challenges them intellectually. In a sense this could be considered as part of the "pay" they receive for their volunteer hours.

So how can a board learning environment be engendered? First, the practice could be established of devoting the first 10-15 minutes of each board meeting to a thought-provoking topic related to the organization's mission and its pursuit of excellence. This could be done simply through a discussion in which board members share their views on the topic and fellow members get challenged to think of the topic in creative and different ways, encouraging them to learn from each other.
Another approach would be to invite a guest speaker to share his/her expertise on a topic related to the governance, programs, or management of the organization. This could be limited to the same ten to fifteen-minute time frame.

Another approach is to provide short articles to board members on topics of interest in the governance, program, and/or management areas. These could be discussed during the education portion of a future meeting where various perspectives on the readings could be shared.

Finally, another approach is having board members attend regional or national conferences or local workshops and report back to the board on a topic that relates to the organization's mission and vision.

Welcome to an Incoming Board Chair

Constance Carter

Author's editorial comment:
Board chairs should be chosen because they are the very best people for the job. Board recruitment should always focus on the strategic goal of selecting members who are or might become excellent leaders.

It's important to avoid the scenario of choosing a board chair because: 1) no one else wanted the job, or 2) the organization had a succession plan whereby the Vice Chair (whose role did not prepare him/her to become Chair) automatically became the Chair. This job is too important. Handled skillfully, the Board Chair can significantly enhance the work of the nonprofit. If seen as an opportunity for power and control, using the "if it ain't broke, break it" mentality, the Chair can undermine an organization, destroy staff morale, and perpetuate a weak, poorly functioning board.

This letter from a fictional outgoing board chair offers some tips about how to navigate this territory successfully.

Congratulations!

Thank you for accepting the position of Chair of the Board of our organization. Since you've been on other boards and on several of our committees, you are familiar with many aspects of our organization, and have a broad view of the work we do.

As Chair of the Board you are the primary liaison between the **board** and the **staff**, specifically the Executive Director. The Board Chair's role is to make sure the board maintains focus on governance, fund raising, planning, and big picture issues.

Our board members are successful professionals with years of experience, and they were recruited specifically because of their expertise and knowledge. But when they enter the board room they do so as unpaid volunteers with a variety of skills who are ultimately responsible for the health and welfare of our nonprofit.

As Chair you conduct board meetings. You set the tone and create an atmosphere conducive to thoughtful, respectful, and engaging discussions. Some chairs choose to use a formal structure, such as Robert's Rules of Order, while others may take a more informal approach. Regardless of the method you choose, it's essential that you ensure meetings begin and end on time, the agenda is completed, and votes are taken as needed.

Board meetings are the members' primary contact with our organization's mission and work. You are responsible for getting updates from the Executive Director and other key staff for each meeting. The Board Chair should minimize time spent reviewing reports and include a substantive discussion about some aspect of governance, policy, or planning in every meeting to keep members energized and thinking creatively.

The Chair should encourage all board members to participate in fund raising in some way. Begin by asking each board member to make a cash gift to the nonprofit that is meaningful to them. The most effective fund raising occurs when the board and staff work as a team. The board must be active in this year-round, not just at annual giving time or when there's an event. It is the Board Chair's job to reinforce that team approach as often as needed.

Periodically I, as Board Chair, had to intervene with board members who became disruptive at meetings, routinely arrived late, missed meetings, or generally didn't seem to be engaged. However, the work our nonprofit did was too important to jeopardize by having a less than committed and effective board. So, with the support of the Governance Committee, we had the conversations; once we even had to ask someone to resign from the board. Thankfully we had board policies and job descriptions in place, which provided leverage and made the whole process simpler and smoother. We also used term limits for board members, which made it easier to "nudge" someone off the board.

The Board Chair must build a strong, trusting, and effective working partnership with the Executive Director. Meet monthly to get regular updates and news, and to discuss new opportunities and problems. These meetings are essential to forge a constructive and successful relationship. We agreed there could be no surprises at board meetings; it was essential that we be open and honest with each other. We prepared the agenda for board meetings, participated with other board members in recruiting and orienting new members, met with funders, and discussed committee work. It's important to note that I did not "meddle" in operational issues or tell her how to do her job. Rather, I was available to her as a resource and a collaborator.

Staff members are keenly aware of what board members say, how they say it, and their support or lack of support for the Executive Director. Always be professional and respectful.

The Chair may choose to delegate the implementation of the Executive Director's annual performance evaluation to the Human Resources Committee, and also participate as a key member in the evaluation process. The same approach is used if another Executive Director search occurs.

Other Considerations
One of the most challenging aspects of the Chair's role is to make sure the board maintains its focus on governance, fund raising, planning, and "big picture" issues while the Executive Director is responsible for the day-to-day activities.

> ➢ The Chair's primary job is to support and further the mission, not to change the organization.
> ➢ The Chair's job is not to micro-manage the Executive Director.
> ➢ The Chair's job is to help the board avoid meddling in operational issues. Any operational recommendations should come to the board from a standing committee. The committee chair should notify the Board Chair in advance if a committee is bringing such a recommendation to a board meeting.

Avail yourself of the excellent and affordable board training workshops in the area and suggest and encourage board members to do the same. Consider bringing in a consultant to the annual board retreat to provide a workshop on a specific topic of need or interest.

Thank you for taking on this very important volunteer job. Hopefully you will find this opportunity to truly make a positive difference and support the work of our nonprofit to be inspiring and challenging.

Sincerely,

The Outgoing Board Chair

When It's Time to Go:
Mentoring and Firing Dysfunctional Board Members

Constance Carter

It's difficult to "fire" a volunteer, but it's more challenging to co-exist with one who is no longer performing the task well or who is being obstructionist or even destructive. Negative, disruptive board members undermine the effectiveness of the board and can make it difficult to recruit new members. As difficult and uncomfortable as it may be to intervene in these situations, it is worse to let them persist.

This is a job for the Board Chair and/or the Governance Committee. The Executive Director can be helpful in identifying dysfunctional or problematic board members and discussing possible interventions, but the task of making a change is a board responsibility. Unfortunately, nonprofit board members often avoid dealing with such situations, to the detriment of the board and the entire organization.

Board members "go bad" for a variety of reasons:

1. **Inadequate vetting and not educating the prospect enough up front about the culture and work of the organization and board member expectations.** Being a board member is a job that includes a variety of skills. One director commented about a board member who was fired, "It became clear after a while that he had a very different mindset from the rest of the board; he was actually becoming belligerent during meetings." Often it takes time for these issues to manifest themselves, and that in itself can make firing someone even harder as time goes by. (For more information on interviewing prospective board members see the essay "Recruiting Board Members: The Right Questions to Ask" in Section IV).

2. **A board member strongly disagrees with a decision the board has made.** It's important to discern whether this is a healthy disagreement that will eventually resolve with discussion, or if the

person is truly unable to put aside the difference and move forward. This scenario can take many forms – from simple negativity, grudge bearing, or refusals to contribute, to one situation where a disgruntled board member even sent letters to the editor of the local newspaper, publicly complaining about the actions of the nonprofit.

3. **The board member's skills are no longer needed on the board, or the organization has matured beyond them.** This scenario can arise when people have served on a board for many years, perhaps even decades, and they are unaware of what is required of board members today. It can also occur in young nonprofits where board members were originally recruited to do hands-on work, such as answering telephones, managing finances, cleaning the offices, or supervising staff. These volunteers generally do not have the expertise in planning, policy, fund raising, and management that are needed as the organization matures. As new board members with higher level skills are recruited, longer term members may dig in and actually try to impede progress. In these scenarios one often hears complaints of "that's how we've always done it," or "we tried that and it didn't work."

The following are three different categories of symptoms of the dysfunctional board member.

1. Significant issues requiring immediate action

➢ Not putting the organization first: not considering the long-run greater good or putting personal interests ahead of the organization's.
➢ Slandering the organization, its programs, staff, or board members, either verbally or in writing.
➢ Disregarding government regulations and laws pertaining to the organization.
➢ Trying to advance themselves, their friends, their business, or relatives through involvement on the board.

- ➤ Being unethical: not recusing when there is an obvious conflict of interest.
- ➤ Misusing organizational resources, especially money.
- ➤ Harassing clients, staff, or other volunteers.
- ➤ Meddling in operations or directing staff.

2. Moderate symptoms that may be resolved by mentoring and coaching
(These symptoms move up to the major category if there is no change after coaching.)

- ➤ Not acknowledging or respecting the current strategic plan and trying to block new initiatives and growth.
- ➤ Not following organizational policies.
- ➤ Being disruptive during meetings by repeatedly arriving late, using cell phones during meetings, being negative, or frequently arguing with the board.
- ➤ Developing cliques, especially ones that pit board members against each other; continually challenging the Executive Director or other stake holders.
- ➤ Refusing to join or chair a standing committee.
- ➤ Not participating in fund raising.
- ➤ Not being a community ambassador.

3. Minor symptoms that can usually be resolved by mentoring and coaching
(These symptoms move up to the moderate category if there is no change after coaching.)

- ➤ Missing more meetings than allowed in the by-laws; not attending specially scheduled meetings.
- ➤ Misusing a committee's responsibility by acting independently and without transparency.
- ➤ Not being prepared for meetings.
- ➤ Not showing appreciation for staff and volunteers.
- ➤ Refusing to make an annual financial contribution to the organization.

Strategies for Managing and/or Removing Dysfunctional Board Members

1. Acknowledge a problem is occurring and agree to address it. This is a conversation for the Board Chair and the Governance Committee, perhaps with input from the Executive Director. Other board members may also need to be involved, depending on their relationships with the problematic member.

2. Develop and then implement a strategy for addressing the situation depending on a variety of variables, such as:

    ➢ the length of time the person has been on the board,
    ➢ when the person's term limit will expire,
    ➢ the culture of the organization and how comfortable people are with exposing and dealing with problems,
    ➢ the intensity and type of problems/issues the person's behavior is causing, and
    ➢ concerns regarding potential fall-out that might arise from removing the person, such as loss of funding or other resources, bad press, or loss of donors.

    (For an example of a policy regarding board member removal, see "Board Member Removal Policy" in the Appendix).

Implementing the Strategy

1. If the Board Chair is willing and has the appropriate skills, enlist him/her to meet privately with the member, discuss the situation, and discern whether the person is interested in changing behaviors or would prefer to leave the board. This can only be successful if the board chair has the willingness and enough self-confidence to directly and clearly address the situation. If the member opts for changing behaviors, the problems must be discussed specifically so he/she clearly knows what is expected.

2. If you can handle the board member for a while longer, wait for his/her term of office to end and do not elect the person to another term. When the current term ends, thank the person for his/her service and say goodbye. As one consultant commented, "A second term is an honor, not a right." This is the least intrusive method of coping with problematic situations and is particularly useful when a board member has served for many years.

3. Enlist another board member to coach or mentor the board member and to intervene if problems arise during board meetings. This can be effective if the two members have a relationship outside of the board, or if they have successfully worked together on behalf of the nonprofit.

4. Use strategic planning to identify new skills needed on the board, and then use that as a rationale to ask someone to leave the board to make room for new members with the necessary skills. For example, "Our new plan shows that we need new board members with strong real estate and construction skills and networks ..."

5. Strategically create a sub-committee of several board members who are aware of the problems to work on a task/project with the problem board member, and to subtly mentor the person throughout the process.

6. Hire a consultant to provide a workshop on roles and responsibilities of nonprofit boards, including discussion about proper meeting behavior. Inform the consultant beforehand that problems are occurring and ask him/her to include content about those specific issues. As follow up to the workshop, appoint a board member to be a "meeting monitor" and agree to have him/her "call out" disruptive behavior when it occurs. This makes the interventions less personal and shifts responsibility to the board as a whole. An additional benefit is that all boards periodically need refresher education about their jobs and the nonprofit's work. The workshop can be educational and inspiring for everyone, in addition to helping address the problem.

7. Empower the Board Chair to institute a practice of reserving five minutes at the end of each board meeting to evaluate the meeting's process and effectiveness. Appoint a different member to facilitate this each time, so the responsibility is shared. Clearly identify situations when problematic behaviors occurred: the discussion got off track, sidebars popped up, cell phones were used, or people were late. Discuss ways to improve the next meeting. (See "Board Meeting Assessment Survey" in the Appendix for a sample meeting evaluation form).

The Board Chair should begin the next meeting by reviewing the issues that occurred at the prior meeting and encouraging more effective behavior.

SECTION V: BOARD OPERATIONS

"Hello, J.G.? I've found a volunteer who's
willing to head up the fund drive!"

Ensuring Effective Nonprofit Boards:
Challenges and Solutions

Part I

Constance Carter

One of the unique features of nonprofit organizations is that a volunteer board of directors supervises a professional Executive Director. Richard Chait, author of Governance as Leadership: Reframing the Work of Nonprofit Boards (Wiley, 2004) stated: "Board members are part-time amateurs overseeing the work of full-time professionals which, by definition, takes a certain amount of hubris." Navigating that potentially conflict-laden structure can be challenging for both groups.

Ideally, nonprofit board members bring a variety of skills, networks, and experience, which either align specifically with the services and programs provided by the organization or are strategically useful in other ways, such as with new business development, marketing, or fund raising. Nonprofit boards should also be diverse demographically and ethnically, reflecting the community served.

However, all too often board members are recruited in response to the question, "who do you know?" rather than through a thoughtful strategic process. As a result, people without any relevant skills may join a board just because a friend asked them. One board member at a local nonprofit once commented, "I joined because my friend asked me and said it would only take an hour a month, and I wouldn't have to do anything."

To make matters worse, boards often lack job descriptions for their members, and/or guidelines and expectations for their performance. Thus, people may agree to join the board without a clear understanding of their responsibilities. Board members may attend meetings unprepared, not having read meeting minutes, reports, or emails sent to them. Others may arrive late or frequently miss meetings. Some consider board meetings as social occasions, and make sidebar observations or off-topic comments, disrupting and confusing the proceedings. Further complicating the situation is the fact that the volunteer board has the power to hire and fire the Executive Director and make policies that may or may not be appropriate.

Another challenge that board members who come from the for-profit world may face is a lack of nonprofit board experience; they may expect a nonprofit board to be similar to that of a for-profit. They often have difficulty understanding the "bottom line" difference – that of mission focus rather than profit. A strong board orientation program, described in Part II of this essay, can help to alleviate the culture shock of moving from the for-profit sector to a nonprofit organization. (For more on this topic see "Learning from Nonprofits and For-Profits" in Section I.)

All these conditions create frustration for the executive staff, whose work at the nonprofit is their full-time profession.

There are several practices a nonprofit organization can adopt to help ease this inherent conflict and ensure that the board is a high-performing group capable of providing inspired leadership in a strong, effective partnership with the Executive Director.

1) Boards need to grow and change as the organization grows.
A new board member often assumes that the board operates just like other boards they may have experienced. However, a hands-on board guiding a new, start-up organization should function differently from a governance-oriented board leading a mature nonprofit. The roles and responsibilities are fundamentally the same, but they are discharged in very different ways. Therefore, it is important for the board and staff leaders to periodically reflect on the nonprofit's growth and status. Is the organization still building its programs and struggling to obtain adequate resources? Is the staff professional and diverse, managing programs that are well respected and successful? Does the nonprofit need people to roll up their sleeves and run events, or does it now need people who can make introductions to potential corporate sponsors?

Nonprofit organizations are affected by changes in public and private funding resources, competition from other organizations, collaborations and mergers, changes in the population served, and regulations and legal issues, among others. Navigating new situations may mean the board periodically needs different skills and networks to be effective. The board may be called upon to play new, varied roles.

Changes need to be clearly identified and recognized. Change is especially challenging when an organization's founder is running the organization or is on the board, or where the board includes members who have served for many years. A healthy nonprofit board will recognize that change is needed and facilitate its progression.

2) The Executive Director and the Board Chair should meet on a regular basis.

The two individuals who have the most influence on the organization are the Chair of the Board and the Executive Director. The Chair is responsible for board meetings and has a major impact on what the board does, through policies and oversight of the operations by the committees of the board. The Executive Director is responsible for the nonprofit's day-to-day operations and ensures the board policies are implemented. Effective and consistent communication is essential for both entities to work well together.

Regularly scheduled monthly meetings featuring respectful dialogue are some of the best ways to build that rapport. These meetings provide opportunities for effective working relationships to be built and maintained, and for each person to share their insights and views. Items arising from board meetings should also be discussed, in addition to a review of finances, the progress of the strategic plan, and any ongoing or new situations.

3) Use a matrix for strategic board and committee recruitment.

One of the simplest ways to ensure the board has the skills and diversity needed to lead the nonprofit is to use a matrix to evaluate the composition of the current board and guide the recruitment of new members. (See the appendix for sample professional and demographic matrices.) This is one of the most effective ways to build qualified and strategically oriented governance groups capable of meeting the organization's needs.

First, convene a diverse group of board and staff to develop a list of the skills, resources, and networks the organization currently needs and will need in the next 3-5 years. Using the strategic plan as a resource, identify programs or initiatives that may require new capabilities not represented by the current board or committee. Using a spreadsheet, list all those functions and characteristics across the top of the matrix. Include demographic and ethnic descriptors and the date when members' terms of office expire, necessitating they retire from the board. This will enable the organization to proactively plan to replace any essential skills.

Second, insert the current board or committee members' names down the left side of the matrix and put check marks in each of the characteristic boxes that apply to each member. Use the unchecked characteristics to guide your recruitment.

Third, see if there are any current members who do not meet the desired qualifications, or where members overlap. Overlapping is not necessarily a problem, especially if the characteristic(s) is especially important. For example, having several board members with capital campaign expertise is not a problem for an organization contemplating or launching a campaign. However, if a large percentage of the members represent a similar skill or characteristic it may indicate a need to diversify. This can be done by asking the member with the least amount of time left on his/her term to leave and make space for someone else with different skills. It could also be accomplished by adding new people to a committee, thereby expanding its capacity and effectiveness.

Ensuring Effective Nonprofit Boards:
Challenges and Solution

Part II

Constance Carter

The following are five additional recommendations about how to ensure a board provides top quality, dynamic leadership.

1) Establish clear guidelines and job descriptions for board and committee members.

Performance guidelines and job descriptions are usually created by the Governance or Nominating Committee to define the behaviors and activities the nonprofit organization expects from the members of its board or committees. A prospective board or committee member can then effectively and thoughtfully decide whether he/she wishes to join and be able to meet the requirements. It can also be a useful tool to ease the difficult situation when asking a member to retire when the current term ends, or when a member needs to be fired due to noncompliance with the guidelines. (See the appendix for a sample Board Member Position Description.)

Minimum guidelines should contain the following:

- ➤ **Expectations concerning meeting attendance**. Include how many meetings will be held per year, how many absences per year are allowed, how many meetings can be attended virtually, etc.
- ➤ **Expectations concerning member behavior**. Include preparation for meetings, responsiveness to e-mails and phone calls in between meetings, cell phone use during meetings, and any other items that may be specific to the nonprofit.
- ➤ **Expectations concerning an annual financial donation.** Define and clarify this policy decision to avoid the situation where a member thinks that just participation on the board or committee is sufficient. Some organizations require a minimum financial

contribution; others ask for a contribution that is personally significant for each member.

> **Expectations concerning other specific requirements.** Faith-based nonprofits may require that members sign a statement of faith or attend a particular religious congregation. Others may require that members participate in or refrain from specific types of activities. Be sure to clearly state what these are, so prospective members can make informed decisions.

The job description should list the tasks board members are expected to fulfill, such as:

> Provide mission-based leadership and strategic governance.
> Participate in the development and implementation of short and long-range strategic plans.
> Provide fiscal oversight.
> Ensure legal and ethical integrity and accountability.
> Participate in fund raising initiatives.
> Advocate for the nonprofit in the community.
> Participate in one or more standing committees.
> Hire, fire, and evaluate the Executive Director.

The Governance Committee should review the guidelines and job description annually with the board, to ensure they continue to be accurate. Boards need to change as the nonprofit grows and adapts to new situations. The guidelines and board job description may also need to change.

2) Establish and abide by term limits for the Board of Directors
One of the simplest, most effective, and diplomatic way to ensure the board continually renews itself is to establish and abide by term limits. However, it is all too common for a board to not adopt this practice or if they do have term limits, to not enforce them.

Term limits mean that board members can serve up to a specific number of terms. The term length is also stated, often two or three years. After the term limit is reached, board members must leave the board for a defined period of time, during which the member may continue to serve the nonprofit organization in another capacity, such as on a standing or ad hoc committee. After that, some organizations allow the person to be considered again for board membership. If a matrix is used to determine if the person's skills continue to be relevant, this decision is made much easier.

Nonprofit organizations that don't use term limits are missing a significant opportunity. They are potentially compromising the organization's ability to grow and thrive by enabling the leadership group to stagnate. These boards typically thwart newcomers from questioning how things are done or introducing new ideas, seriously compromising the quality of oversight and frustrating new members.

Staggering the term limits ensures that board members rotate off at different times, thus making board recruitment a year-round, manageable activity with reasonable goals and timeframes. Another benefit of term limits is they allow a nonprofit to proactively plan for a key member's departure. Finding that person's replacement may take time and needs to be done thoughtfully. Term limits also make it easier for a board member to gracefully exit a board, a task that is often difficult for people who do not want to offend the group. (For more on this topic see the article "The Importance of Term Limits" in section IV.)

3) No nepotism.
In the nonprofit world nepotism is not a Best Practice, even though it is a well-accepted practice in for-profit family-run businesses. Rather than strategically and deliberately recruiting skilled, qualified staff and/or board members, nonprofit leaders who enlist their family members court negative consequences.

The IRS 990 form contains a question designed to catch and highlight any family or business relationships existing among officers, directors, trustees, or key employees. Many funders will not make grants to organizations where these types of relationships are present, regardless of the strategies that may be used to try and make the situation appear less harmful or even benign.

Coping with nepotism becomes even more difficult when an organization may have been founded by a family and one or more family members is on the board and/or staff. The simplest way to manage it is to never let it happen, by ensuring there are organizational and board policies to prevent it. For an organization already compromised with such an arrangement, it should be openly addressed and eliminated, regardless of how attractive and/or compelling the relationships are.

4) Develop a robust, comprehensive board orientation process for new members.
One board member commented recently, "When I joined the board, I really didn't understand what the issues were or what I could do to help. I'd read the materials sent to me, but I was reluctant to ask questions or participate in the discussions because I was so new, and I didn't want to slow everything down with my lack of experience. It took me six months to feel I was contributing at all."

That comment is not unusual but is fairly easy to address.

The Governance Committee of the board should develop and implement a policy concerning how new members are welcomed to the board (or committee) and educated about the organization and their specific responsibilities as members. At a minimum, the policy should include:

> *A board manual.* The manual should include the board job description and responsibilities, by-laws, articles of incorporation, contact information for board and committee members and key staff, organizational chart, most recent audit and IRS 990 report, current and prior year budgets, and the strategic plan. Any other items that might be helpful to the new member should be included as well, such as brochures, press releases, etc. (See the appendix for a sample manual table of contents).

> *Assigning each new board member a current board member as a mentor for nine-12 months.* The mentor should review and discuss meeting agendas and materials with the new member and be available to answer questions between meetings. These conversations provide opportunities for in-depth discussions about

issues confronting the board and give the new member much-needed background and history.

➤ ***Ensuring the new board member visits the organization regularly during his/her first year on the board, and at least annually thereafter.*** This is especially important if board meetings are not held during regular business hours, or if they are held off-site.

5) Confidentiality

The nonprofit world recognizes three basic duties of board members: Duty of Care, Duty of Loyalty, and Duty of Obedience. The Duty of Loyalty includes respecting the confidentiality of the organization's business. Quite simply, items discussed in the board room need to stay in the board room. All board members need to understand that meeting topics should remain confidential, unless there is a clearly stated agreement that information may be shared. This needs to be regularly reinforced at board meetings, as it's easy for members to forget. If an organization's board meetings are open to visitors, topics requiring confidentiality should be handled during a separate part of the meeting that is closed to non-board members.

Nuts and Bolts of Effective Board Meetings

Constance Carter

*"Do your little bit of good where you are; it's those little
bits of good put together that overwhelm the world."*
Desmond Tutu

Most people join a nonprofit board because they care deeply about the
work the organization does. They want to donate their time, money, and
talent to ensure its success. They want to make a contribution and know
that their involvement makes a difference.

One of the primary ways board members demonstrate their involvement is
through participating in board meetings. It is, therefore, essential that
board meetings be inspiring, timely, and effective, involving substantive
discussions about strategic issues that impact the organization and its
work. At each meeting's conclusion, members should feel that their time
was well spent, and their input and presence were valued.

Here are five tips to ensuring these outcomes occur.

1. Meeting Frequency and Scheduling
An organization's by-laws state the number of board meetings required
each year. Four-six meetings per year are sufficient for most
organizations, although more frequent meetings may be necessary for a
new organization or one facing significant change. Some boards prefer to
not meet during the summer or year-end holidays; others may vary the
schedule depending on the organization's activities. For example, a
summer music festival board might need to meet more often before and
during the summer and skip a winter meeting.

Scheduling board meetings should be determined by the board members,
not the staff, and the schedule should periodically be reevaluated as new
people join the board. Meeting schedules are often key factors in
determining whether a prospective member is able to join the board. For
example, younger people may not have the flexibility that older members

have regarding taking time off from work to attend board meetings. Those with young children or older adult members may not want to attend evening meetings. Boards that demonstrate some flexibility regarding this issue will be better positioned to recruit diverse members who have the skills and resources the organization needs.

Distribute the yearly board meeting schedule at the beginning of each year, ensuring all members include the meetings on their calendars well in advance.

2. Plan and Conduct Inspiring and Efficient Board Meetings
The Board Chair and the Executive Director should meet in advance of each board meeting to discuss and plan the agenda, utilizing input from committees and staff, including issues raised from previous board meetings that need consideration, and any new items. Board meetings should start and end promptly, and last no longer than two hours. There is no quicker way to alienate and frustrate board members than to keep them waiting for late comers, or to let a meeting run overtime. Consistently implementing a board culture regarding punctuality is vital to the success of the board.

Most meeting agendas should include the following:

> ➢ Reading of the mission and values statements. This helps keep members focused on the work and reminds them why they are there and how important their volunteerism is.
> ➢ Review and approval of the last meeting's minutes, noting any changes.
> ➢ Comments by the Board Chair concerning issues that have occurred since the last meeting.
> ➢ Committee reports.
> ➢ A review of the current portion of the strategic plan. This will help ensure the plan is accomplished in a timely way.
> ➢ The Executive Director's report.
> ➢ Discussion about a substantive item, such as a new policy, issue, change, challenge, or opportunity.

3. Consent Agenda and Committee Reports: Keeping the board meetings fresh, interesting, and strategic

A consent agenda combines routine business, staff, and committee reports into one agenda item that can be approved in one action. High performing boards often use this process to save time, provide opportunities for in-depth discussion of issues, and keep people engaged. The consent agenda moves these routine items along quickly, eliminating the need for time consuming reports that are often repetitive and dry.

Items that work well in a consent agenda format are non-controversial or routine items, such as meeting minutes, the Executive Director's report, and committee reports (with the exception of the finance report, which generally requires a hands-on review at each meeting). The Board Chair and Executive Director take the lead in implementing a consent agenda, distributing the meeting agenda and relevant reports to the board well in advance of the meeting.

The consent agenda concept is not appropriate for all boards, for several reasons:

> ➤ All board members must regularly commit to reading the materials beforehand. If board members typically do not read or respond to e-mails, or tend to come to meetings unprepared, the consent agenda is not an option.
> ➤ Board members need to take responsibility to ask questions either in advance or during the meeting about any items in the reports they question or don't understand. The consent agenda is not a strategy to facilitate "rubber stamping" acceptance of reports. Controversial or significant items will still need adequate review and discussion.
> ➤ The committees must be functioning effectively, and other board members need to trust their work is high quality and meeting the nonprofit's needs. The board should discuss the mission and work of each committee annually to be sure it continues to be relevant.
> ➤ Committee meetings need to be held far enough in advance of the board meeting so there is sufficient time for minutes and other materials to be prepared. For example, hold the board meeting

toward the end of the month and committee meetings the first or second week of the month.

4. Manage Cliques, Sidebars, and other Distractions
One of the Board Chair's most challenging tasks is to manage the flow and effectiveness of a board meeting. This responsibility is essential in order to cover the agenda items and keep members engaged. Distracting behaviors such as interruptions, off-topic discussions, sidebar conversations, checking a cell phone, or texting during meetings can be extremely disruptive. The board chair must respectfully yet firmly address these actions, during or after the meeting.

Some boards develop policies about cell phone use during meetings; others include a statement about cell phone use at the beginning of each meeting.

Cliques can occur when several board members discuss issues outside the confines of a meeting. This may polarize a board when everyone is not included in these conversations, resulting in different factions taking predetermined positions, without full group discussion. These situations are difficult to prevent, as board members may be friends or colleagues who socialize between meetings. Identifying and controlling them in a board meeting is the responsibility of the Board Chair.

5. Periodically evaluate a board meeting.
Once or twice a year The Governance Committee should ask the board to complete a post-board meeting evaluation. The evaluation should ask questions about how effective the meeting was, the quality of the discussion, whether he/she participated in the discussion, and whether the member felt the meeting was a good use of his/her time. (See the appendix for a sample evaluation form). The results of the evaluation should be reviewed by the Governance Committee and by the full board at the next board meeting. If issues have been identified, include a discussion about how to make changes to improve the quality of the meetings.

Standing Board Committees

Constance Carter

"Alone we can do so little - together we can do so much."
Helen Keller

Benefits of Standing Committees

A full roster of effective board standing committees is a common characteristic of high performing nonprofit organizations. These groups are staffed with professionals, usually three to ten, with expertise in the area of the committee's oversight and contribute significantly to the functioning and success of the nonprofit.

Standing committee meetings increase the efficiency of the Board of Directors, as they provide opportunities for in-depth discussion and evaluation of specific issues that are not feasible in a board meeting, enabling the board to focus on policy and planning responsibilities.

Committees provide opportunities to recruit new people. Such individuals might not choose to join the board, due to the time commitment, fiduciary and/or legal responsibilities involved with board membership. Likewise, when someone joins a committee, the board and staff have opportunities to observe the person "in action," and determine if the person might eventually be a strong board member. The committee member will have a chance to learn more about the organization and its operations and will be able to make a more informed decision if asked to join the board.

Committee membership provides unique volunteer leadership opportunities for younger people getting started in their careers, as well as opportunities for them to benefit from participating in a professional group with more experienced people. Many nonprofits today are keenly aware of the need to engage with those under 40 in meaningful ways, and committee membership is an excellent way to do this.

Standing committees expand a nonprofit's network, as every committee member brings new resources and connections. One Board Chair commented, "Our fund raising and public relations efforts really took off once we expanded our standing committees with non-board members. We were able to get access to so many new people, businesses, and organizations, and that ultimately enabled us to run a successful capital campaign. I don't think that would have been possible without those committee members, because our board was pretty small."

Standing Committee Management

Ideally, each committee should be chaired by a board member. This provides a direct link between the committee and the board, ensuring smooth communication between both groups.

Committees typically do not make decisions unless empowered by the board to do so. Their role is to study, discuss, and recommend; it is the committee chair's responsibility to bring recommendations to the board for further action. When the chair is a board member that process is facilitated.

Committees bring many benefits, and they do consume staff time and require management. The Executive Director and/or a staff member who is involved in the work of the committee should attend each meeting, to provide information and support, and to keep the committee focused on the task at hand. This time commitment is often the reason Executive Directors cite in justifying why they don't have multiple committees: lack of time or energy. However, the benefits a strategically recruited, effective committee can bring far outweigh the costs.

Characteristics of Effective Committees

➤ They have a clear purpose/mission and a well-defined job description codified in a charter. (For more on this topic see "Importance of Board Committee Charters" in Section V and the sample committee charter in the appendix.)

- Committee member qualifications, skills and networks are specified.
- They utilize goals and timelines for their work, based on priorities in the strategic plan.
- The committee chair, in collaboration with appropriate staff, develops an agenda for each meeting.
- Minutes are prepared and sent to members in advance of each meeting; minutes may also be sent to board members for their information.
- They establish an annual meeting schedule and adhere to it. The Finance Committee should meet monthly; others usually meet at least 4 times/year, and sometimes more often, depending on the work being done and its urgency.
- The committee chair briefly reports on the committee's work at each board meeting to keep the board informed and ensure the committee is meeting the board's expectations.
- All committee members should make an annual cash contribution to the organization and support fund raising activities.

A Word of Caution

Because committees are charged with delving more deeply into specific aspects of the operations of the nonprofit than the board does, it's easy for a committee to get too hands on and slide into a habit of micromanaging staff. This is not the purpose of a committee.

Depending on the size of the organization and the support needed from the committee, members may be asked at times to help with jobs typically done by staff, such as addressing letters, meeting with auditors, interviewing consultants, etc. This can be very useful – however, it can be a slippery slope if such activities become routine and assumed. The committee chair needs to pay careful attention to be sure members are acting in appropriate ways within the committee's mandate.

Committees and Their Primary Functions

It is considered best practice for all nonprofits to have at least Executive, Governance, and Finance committees. Because most nonprofits rely heavily on fundraising revenues, a fundraising committee is also extremely important. Below is a brief description of some of the most common standing committees, in order of priority. The appendix contains a sample committee charter that can be adapted to fit a specific committee.

Governance

This is one of the most important board committees, if not the most important. In collaboration with the Board Chair, the committee's scope includes recruitment and oversight of the Board of Directors, its composition, functioning, health, and wellbeing. In some organizations this committee is also responsible for the committee structure and ensuring there are adequate and appropriate members.

Executive

The Executive Committee's primary function is to act for the board when something arises requiring a quick response or action. Typically, this committee comprises the officers of the board. Some organizations also include several other members or key committee chairs. A board member may also be asked to participate in an Executive Committee meeting if he/she has specific expertise or input concerning a topic being discussed. They can also be used for in-depth discussions of specific issues when there isn't a strong committee structure. In these instances, the committee may make a decision itself or recommend action to the board.

My recommendation is that Executive Committees should only meet when absolutely necessary. Here's why:

> ➢ If the committee meets frequently, it may make too many decisions in its role of acting for the board. In these instances, the board may feel they are merely rubberstamping decisions made by the committee. It is essential the board remains aware of how the committee is functioning, and ensure it only meets when needed.

➤ The Executive Committee can also be misused to compensate for a weak or ineffective board. In those instances, the most functional members of the board form the Executive Committee, and basically do an "end run" around the board when making decisions. This perpetuates the board's dysfunction. The solution here is to fix the board, not delegate to the Executive Committee.
➤ With today's technology, such as free conference calls and internet-based meeting platforms, it is easier than ever to assemble a quorum in an emergency situation, rather than resort to using the Executive Committee.

Finance
This committee provides oversight of the organization's finances, policies, investments, and overall fiscal health. The committee is responsible for sending the board timely, accurate, and easy to understand financial reports prior to each board meeting. It ensures that the board has the skills to interpret these reports, and that their questions and concerns are addressed.

Audit
Although many nonprofit organizations consider managing the audit to be part of the Finance Committee's responsibilities, today it is considered a best practice to establish a separate Audit Committee. This provides an additional level of scrutiny and oversight of the audit process. The committee should recommend a selection of an auditor to the board, ensuring that the process is thorough and transparent. The committee meets with the auditor and reviews the auditor's report before it goes to the Finance Committee.

Personnel or Human Resources
Unless an organization has only a few employees, this is an essential committee. The primary purview of the committee is to review benefits, raises, and employment practices along with ensuring the personnel policies are up to date and reviewed periodically. The committee also oversees the Executive Director's annual evaluation and provides consultation and support to the Executive Director regarding personnel issues or concerns.

Volunteers also come under the Personnel Committee's purview. This includes compiling and updating the volunteer handbook and ensuring the organization is in compliance with all legal regulations concerning volunteers.

Development or Fundraising

Development committees oversee the creation and implementation of the annual development plan, in collaboration with staff. This committee can significantly enhance an organization's fundraising capacity if the members are recruited strategically with a focus on their networks, skills, and willingness to cultivate and solicit donors. Choosing members who have access to potential donors, corporations, and foundations and who are willing to make introductions and promote the nonprofit will significantly supplement the work that staff can do.

A Development Committee should only spend a small portion of its time on special fundraising events. Rather, an ad hoc sub-committee of the Development Committee should be formed to work on an event. This provides an opportunity to recruit new volunteers (who will also bring their own networks) who are enthusiastic about event planning, thereby ensuring the Development Committee's work of networking, cultivating, and soliciting donors continues and doesn't get derailed by an event.

Marketing or Public Relations

Although these tasks are often included in a Development Committee's charter because fund raising and marketing/PR are so closely aligned, a separate committee able to focus just on outreach may be helpful, especially if an organization's work relies heavily on communications initiatives. Social media, more traditional media relations, publications, promotional activities, and speaking engagements all fall under the purview of this committee.

Facilities

This committee provides oversight, advice, and support for staff who are responsible for building improvements and maintenance. It is useful if an organization has a physical plant and/or grounds, or several sites. This includes large facility-based organizations, such as hospitals, long term care facilities, schools, and cultural institutions, down to smaller nonprofits that may own a building or two.

Input and oversight of this committee are particularly important in organizations where facility-related expenses represent significant budget line items. Members' professional networks can be extremely helpful in providing access to specialized consultants and contractors.

Programs
Program Committees monitor, measure, and evaluate current programs, oversee new program development, and ensure that the organization's programs are consistent with the mission and strategic plan. These essential activities are required today by many donors and funders.

Additional Possibilities
Ad hoc committees may be established for specific needs the organization may have, such as evaluating new ideas or opportunities or for time-limited projects, such as strategic planning or a capital campaign. Typically, the Executive Director and the Board of Directors will initiate the forming of additional committees.

The Importance of Committee Charters

Louis J. Beccaria

What Is a Charter?

According to the <u>Encyclopedia Britannica</u> a charter "is a document granting certain specified powers, rights, privileges, obligations, or functions from the sovereign power of a state to an individual, corporation, city, or other unit of local organization."

As an overall concept applied to the nonprofit sector, the above definition applies 100%. We know that a well-run nonprofit organization should have a number of committees to help carry out the overall mission of the organization. Some of the more common and essential board committees employed as a matter of best practices are: executive, governance, finance/budget, human resources, fund development/fundraising, and audit committees. (For more information on this topic see "Standing Board Committees" in Section V.)

As it applies to a nonprofit organization, a charter's purpose is to describe the rationale for a board committee as well as its goals and participants. It gives direction and aligns the expectations of the committee members so that their energies are focused on a set of committee priorities.

Essential Elements of a Committee Charter

Mission Statement: Very simply, this is the statement of why the committee exists – its reason for being. If the organization's by-laws or board of directors has deemed it necessary to have certain committees, then it is important to bestow upon these committees the proper structure and visible credibility they are due. It would be difficult for committees to function well if they lacked guidance and did not know why they were in business, so to speak!

Committee Membership: This section notes who has the authority to appoint the committee members. In most cases, the board chair does the appointing. One major reason is that these committees assist the board chair to provide governance leadership for the organization. Another reason for defining the committee's membership is that joining a committee gives board members the opportunity to actively participate and offer their expertise to help accomplish the organization's mission. It is well-known as a matter of best practice that each board member should participate on at least one committee as a means of being active and providing expertise. Conversely, this section of the charter should state that since the board chair has the authority to appoint board members to the committees, he/she also has the authority to remove them.

This membership section of a charter should also indicate the number of people who can participate on the committee. While committees are entities of a board and its membership, it is considered a matter of best practice (that is becoming more common today), to invite community members who are not board members of the organization to sit on committees. The primary benefit this provides is input and wisdom that may represent demographics, expertise, and a voice of diversity not currently available on the board.

Another benefit is that committees can act as a training ground and a "tryout area," if you will, for people who may express an interest in the organization and its mission. Committee participation can be a means to see if there is a good fit for both them and the organization in terms of personality, group chemistry, and active, committed participation. In most cases of which we are aware, community committee participants have the authority to vote on matters discussed in the committees. This gives meaning to their valuable volunteer time and expertise and provides justification for the reason they have been invited to join an organization's committee.

Authority: The organization's by-laws often state what authority board committees actually have. In almost all cases, the usual limit on a committee's authority is that of only providing policy, procedure, or program recommendations to the board for its consideration. Thus, committees almost always do not have the authority to make final decisions on any matter. The recommendations stemming from the committee's deliberations must be brought to the full board for discussion, adoption, or disapproval.

Responsibility: This section of a board committee charter is often the longest and the most important. It provides a list of the exact expectations, goals, and objectives that the board of directors intends for the committee to fulfill. Taking its direction from the committee's statement of mission, this charter section delves deeper to provide specific guidance, direction, and detail about the breadth and limitations of the committee's duties.

In my opinion, it is also a matter of good practice to establish one to three practical and doable goals each year in the committee's area of responsibility to help the organization along in its journey of achieving its mission. This practice provides a better means of overall committee accountability to the board in general and the chair in particular.

Meeting Frequency: As a part of its stated responsibilities, this charter section should note how often the committee must report to the full board on its activities. Reporting frequency could be at each board meeting, once a quarter, semi-annually – whatever the organization believes is most adequate and helpful in moving itself forward.

Charter Authorization: Once the above sections have been developed and agreed upon by the board of directors, each committee charter should be signed by the board chair and the Governance Committee chair. This practice gives visibility to the credibility and seriousness of this policy document. Make no mistake about it, committee charters ARE, in fact, policy documents.

In summary, as a matter of good practice each board committee's charter should be reviewed for its relevance by the organization's Governance Committee at least every three to four years. This does not mean that the charters need to be changed. It merely means that the charters should be reviewed periodically. As time goes by, the needs of an organization may change and, therefore, the responsibilities of various chartered committees might need to change as well.

Nonprofit Boards We've Known:
The Good, The Bad, and the Ugly

Constance Carter

"A strategic board has a view of looking ahead, an insight to look deeper, and competency to look beyond."
Pearl Zhu

A nonprofit board of directors is responsible for providing effective governance, leadership, and planning, and ensuring the organization's sustainability through fiscal and legal oversight and resource development. Because the board of directors can be so helpful in ensuring the health, success, and survival of a nonprofit organization, it is extremely important to pay attention to how well the board functions, identifies problems, and fixes them before they become more serious. Identifying the issues before they become a danger to the organization is vital. This can be difficult as changes are often subtle and occur over time. Below is a description of three basic types of boards, and their characteristics and challenges, along with strategies for fixing them when problems arise.

The good news is that many times, solutions are not that far away, *if people are willing to take action and have the ability to change.*

THE GOOD: HIGH PERFORMING BOARDS

High performing quality organizations that effectively and creatively fulfill their missions typically have high performing boards of directors. Such boards hire dynamic, professional CEOs who respect, understand, and skillfully manage the staff/board partnership to ensure success. These organizations usually have successful, diverse fundraising programs resulting from strong board/staff collaborations that ensure adequate resources are available. The boards are willing to embrace change when necessary, take calculated and thoughtful risks, and invest in new solutions to old problems.

Characteristics

- Full attendance at board meetings. Meetings are characterized by respectful, dynamic discussions and creative brainstorming for solutions to problems.
- Many use a consent agenda model to promote efficiency and encourage interesting discussions. (For more details about this model see "Nuts and Bolts of Effective Board Meetings" in Section V.)
- Members read and respond to e-mails and return phone calls. They come to meetings having read the materials sent to them and are prepared to thoughtfully discuss the agenda items.
- Members are available to each other and the CEO between meetings.
- All members willingly and effectively participate in fundraising and advocate for the organization throughout the year.
- Members have a solid understanding of their roles and responsibilities as board members as well as the difference between the roles of the board and the CEO.
- Members are interested in learning about the organization and how to be more effective.
- People want to join these boards, as members feel a high degree of satisfaction that their time is well spent, and they know they are making a difference.

Challenges

One of the biggest challenges is maintaining the board's effectiveness as terms of office expire, new people join the board, and CEOs change. Keeping the work fresh can also be a challenge, as many nonprofits' work tends to be cyclical or even routine.

Solutions

- Institutionalize how the high performing board functions by developing policies and procedures for how the board operates, and job descriptions for board positions that include clear expectations for members.

➤ Ensure the Governance/Nominating Committee meets year-round and takes an active role in proactively recruiting new members with needed skills and resources to the board and the standing committees. Succession planning for key board leaders and developing board leadership should also be priorities, to ensure continuity.

➤ Promote a learning environment/culture with educational opportunities, workshops, and guest speakers on relevant topics to provide stimulation and new ideas.

➤ Ensure the annual board retreat continues to be an interesting and inspiring event.

THE BAD: INEFFECTIVE, OBSTRUCTIONIST BOARDS

These boards come in all shapes and sizes and, as a result, it can be difficult to identify them at first glance. Often, they embrace an attitude of maintaining the status quo. Other habits and behaviors include procrastinating, inability to make decisions, resisting change, and rubber-stamping reports generated by others. These groups fail to see that not making a decision is really making a decision not to do anything.

Organizations with ineffective boards routinely struggle to obtain the resources they need. They may have community reputations of being stuck in the past, resisting change and new opportunities/collaborations, as well as being unapproachable with new ideas.

Characteristics

➤ Attendance at board meetings is spotty; quorums are not always reached.

➤ Many members may come to meetings not having read pre-meeting materials and thus aren't prepared. Meeting time is then spent reviewing the documents rather than on meaningful discussions.

- Discussions may be dominated by focusing on the past, stating reasons new strategies will not work, and a general sense of indifference.
- While the board's by-laws may include terms of office, they are not enforced. There may be members who have served for 10, 15, or 20 years or more.
- Most board members resist participating in fund raising or outreach activities, viewing it as a staff responsibility. Or they may only be willing to do "what we've always done," usually ineffective special events that consume significant human and cash resources while producing little return.
- Meetings tend to include personal discussions and sidebars between members, creating distractions and wasting time.
- Members often confuse board and CEO roles, meddle in operational issues, and attempt to micro-manage the CEO and/or staff.

Challenges

These boards will stifle and frustrate a dynamic professional CEO by their resistance to change and lack of initiative. For example, one organization's board treasurer, who had been on the board for many years, was allowed to maintain a stranglehold on the organization's financial reserves. This made it impossible for the CEO to implement new programs, even though the funds had been donated and saved for those purposes. Several other organizations suffered with the opposite: those boards happily spent the reserves, funding ongoing annual deficits rather than developing new strategies to correct the problems and ensure financial sustainability. Their attitudes were "we're doing good this way, and if the money runs out, we'll close up and sell."

Solutions

In order for change to occur, several members and the CEO need to understand the problems and be motivated and willing to cope with the inevitable resistance of the other members. This may take some time to accomplish.

- Concerned members and the CEO can ask for help from a consultant or a member of another board who is experienced in helping to rejuvenate under-performing boards. An unbiased third party can provide a fresh vision for solving old problems, and there are many consultants and associations available to provide support.
- Review the by-laws, and, if necessary, update or add terms of office, *and then enforce them.* Ask board members whose attendance is poor or who are particularly ineffective or problematic to rotate off. Some members who are threatened by the changes may choose to leave, and their resignations should be accepted as part of the process. (For more information on this topic see "Board Member Term Limits" in Section IV.)
- As soon as possible, build a Governance/Nominating Committee to identify the skills and resources needed on the board and then recruit new members. (For more information on this topic see "Ensuring Effective Boards Parts I & II" in Section V and the Sample Board Matrices in the Appendix.)
- Prepare a board self-evaluation to identify educational opportunities that members would be willing to embrace and provide them on a regular basis. (See the Appendix for a sample evaluation form.)
- Adopt detailed new protocols for board meetings to eliminate the disruptions and emphasize the importance of reviewing materials before meetings. Include topics on the agenda that are strategic and foster creative conversations.
- Work with each board member to develop an individual fundraising plan and help each person to implement it. If the member is unwilling or unable to do this, ask them to leave the board and join a non-fundraising related standing committee instead. This may sound harsh, but you don't have time to lose! *The survival of the organization depends on this.*

THE UGLY: DYSFUNCTIONAL and DESTRUCTIVE BOARDS – or, as the comedian Ron White says – You Can't Fix Stupid

These boards embrace many of the characteristics of the ineffective, obstructionist boards described above, but to a greater degree. As a result, they are far more dangerous to the survival of the nonprofit. Generally, such boards have existed as an increasingly dysfunctional group for a long time. Members have served for years, know each other fairly well, and the "group think" blocks different or opposing viewpoints. Members believe they are "doing good" simply by being on the board, but don't understand that being a board member is a serious job with significant responsibilities: *the survival and sustainability of the nonprofit are at stake.*

Characteristics

> ➤ These boards resist change and are unable to think outside the box or consider new strategies. They are incapable of making thoughtful decisions or providing leadership. In short, these boards lack a learning culture that should be fostered by the board leadership.
> ➤ Meetings may be filled with reviewing and rubber-stamping reports produced by staff or committees with little or no understanding, action, or initiative taken by the board.
> ➤ Board recruitment is often neglected, leaving gaps in the skills, resources, and diversity that are needed for a more effective governing group. As most members are performing poorly, the board is resistant to asking a disruptive or even unethical board member to resign.
> ➤ New board members may quickly become discouraged with the lack of leadership, negativity, and indifference, and then quit.
> ➤ Often these organizations have few, if any, standing committees, blaming difficulty in recruiting members as the reason. If committees do exist, non-board members are rarely included, thereby ensuring the board maintains control, perpetuating the dysfunction.

> The board may have a negative reputation in the community as being an ineffective group that makes poor decisions.
> The board is highly resistant to fundraising, usually stating "I don't know anyone" or "no one is interested in this nonprofit."
> Some members may arbitrarily insist that operational decisions or changes be made without the CEO's consent and input. This attitude makes it appear that the board is actually doing something, when in reality what they are doing is destructive and counterproductive.

Challenges

As in the bad board scenario described above, the dysfunctional board's inactivity, negativity, poor communication, and operational meddling will quickly frustrate a competent CEO, resulting in turnover and lack of leadership. And, since the board is often responsible for hiring the new CEO, poor choices may be made in choosing a replacement.

There also may be misplaced loyalty and trust in either the CEO or key board members or both, leading to serious problems that go unaddressed for months or years until disaster strikes. One board of an organization with a 230-year old mission of serving low-income seniors met for 15 months without receiving finance reports because they trusted the CEO when she gave somewhat plausible explanations for their absence. They finally woke up to find the organization was in such a dire financial situation that it could not be fixed. The CEO was fired and consultants were brought in, but ultimately the organization was taken over by a for-profit business that served wealthy people. ***The two centuries+ mission and tradition were lost forever.***

One or two board members can inappropriately influence a weak board. Certain members may be considered to be more knowledgeable than others, have more prestige, or be viewed as a "weighty" member because of a job, length of service on the board, community activity, or political affiliation. People may try to control the board meeting and manipulate or monopolize discussions. A strong Board Chair is needed to control these individuals and their attempts to take over, and when the Chair is ineffective, this intervention will be lacking.

There may also be cliques on the board, where members are so trusting of each other that they disregard flagrant fiscal or ethical violations. One Board Chair mishandled funds several times. When the situation was exposed, the board broke into factions: a small group insisted the Board Bhair resign, while the majority reacted with "it's no big deal – we trust him and know he didn't mean it." (For more on this subject see "The Importance of Ethics" in Section I.)

Solutions

These boards are so damaged and damaging that they are basically beyond repair. (As noted above, you can't fix stupid.) A majority of the board members will need to leave before improvements can occur. A CEO change may also be needed at some point during the process. Many of the solutions noted above for ineffective, obstructionist boards will then apply, beginning with hiring a consultant or a member of another board who is experienced in helping to re-build boards. Once the board is restored, it will be important to develop and then implement a new strategic plan to provide guidance, focus, and structure.

APPENDIX

Please contact us for digital copies of any of the following documents.

Louis J. Beccaria: bbguy1945@outlook.com
Constance Carter: ccarter@sylviacarter.com

TABLE OF CONTENTS FOR A BOARD HANDBOOK

Section 1: The Board of Directors
- Statement of Board member responsibilities
- List of Board of Directors and contact information
- List of Board members and their respective terms
- List of committees and their charters
- List of committee members and contact information
- Most recent Board self-evaluation
- Board Member Removal Policy

Section 2: Historical References
- History of the Organization
- Articles of Incorporation
- By-Laws
- IRS 501(c)(3) Tax-Exemption Determination Letter

Section 3: Strategic Framework
- Mission, vision, and values
- Current Strategic Plan
- List of programs with a brief summary of each

Section 4: Finances
- Most recent annual report
- Most recent financial audit
- Most recent IRS Form 990
- Current annual operating budget
- Banking resolutions
- Policies related to investments, reserves, endowments, etc.
- Risk management policies (e.g. Directors & Officers Insurance)

Section 5: Board Governance-Related Policies
- Conflict of Interest Policy
- Whistle Blower Policy
- Document Retention/Destruction Policy
- CEO Succession Procedure

- ➢ Business Insurance Coverage
- ➢ Travel and Meeting Expense Reimbursement Policy
- ➢ Accreditation Documents, if applicable
- ➢ Non-discrimination Policy
- ➢ Harassment Policy
- ➢ Business Recovery Plan

Section 6: Staff
- ➢ Staff job descriptions
- ➢ Employment policies
- ➢ Staff organizational chart

Section 7: Resource Development
- ➢ Case Statement
- ➢ Current funder list (foundations; businesses; major donors)
- ➢ Sponsorship Policy
- ➢ Gift Solicitation and Acceptance Policy
- ➢ Gift Acknowledgement Policy
- ➢ Donor Bill of Rights Policy
- ➢ Policy on Sharing Donor Information

Section 8: Other Information
- ➢ Website
- ➢ Current brochures any other printed materials

FINANCE COMMITTEE CHARTER

MISSION
To monitor the financial performance of the organization's annual operating budget, capital improvement budget, and the solvency of the organization's overall assets.

MEMBERSHIP
The Board chairperson shall appoint three Board members with financial training
and expertise, and up to two non-board member community representatives, if desired.

AUTHORITY
As noted in the organization's by-laws, this committee, as all others of the Board, shall have the authority only to provide policy, procedure, or program recommendations within the mission of this committee. These recommendations shall be brought to the full Board for discussion and consideration for approval.

RESPONSIBILITIES
1. Report to the Board at each regular meeting on financial matters.
2. Make recommendations to the Board re: operational/capital budget matters.
3. Work with the Executive Director in preparing the annual operating budget and present it to the Board for approval.
4. Report to the Board any financial irregularities or concerns regarding compliance issues.
5. Develop/recommend policies/strategies re: investment of the organization's funds to the Board for adoption.
6. Monitor the organization's operation and capital budget expenses as well as its investment performance.
7. Ensure prompt generation of periodic financial statements for Board review.

MEETINGS
This committee shall meet no less than twice a year and as often as needed to deal with any specific situations that may arise in the course of the organization's fiscal year.

Name:_____   Name:_____
        Board Chair   Governance Committee Chair

Date: _____   Date:_____

BOARD PROFESSIONAL AND DEMOGRAPHIC MATRICES

This will be easier to do in an Excel worksheet, but we are offering these as examples of how to create and use matrices to build a strategic, diverse board in an organized manner.

List your current board members' names across the top.

To build a professional matrix, list in the rows down the left the skills or networks needed to ensure a competent and diverse board for the organization. We have included a sampling of some of the basic skills needed on most nonprofit boards. Add in other desired skills which are specific to the organization, such as education, health, mental health, environmental expertise, historical knowledge, etc.

Place a checkmark in the boxes that apply to a particular member.

Once completed, the boxes with few or no checkmarks indicate priority skills that need to be added to the board.

PROFESSIONAL EXPERIENCE MATRIX

Members' Names									
Finance									
Fundraising									
Personnel									
Volunteers									
Management									
Marketing									
Legal									
Programs									
Technology									
Other									
Other									
Other									

DEMOGRAPHICS MATRIX

We recommend using a second matrix for analyzing demographic categories such as gender, race, age, or where a person lives or works, if geographic diversity is important for the organization. We have included a sampling of some of the more common categories nonprofits should consider.

Members' Names									
Under 25									
25-44									
45-59									
Over 60									
Male									
Female									
Asian									
Black									
White									
Latino/a									
Native American									
Other									
Other									
Other									

CRITERIA FOR BOARD CANDIDATES AND CHAIRPERSONS

Board Candidates should have as many of the following as possible:

Personal Characteristics

*Smart/Insightful
*Energetic
*Foresight
*Good Judgment
*Time to Donate to the Job

*Heart for Philanthropy/Cause
*Money to Give
*Good Organizational Skills
*Have Fresh Ideas/Thinking
*Willingness to Work

Professional Characteristics

*Business Sense
*Leadership Skills
*Analytical Skills
*Knowledge and Insight

*Status and Prominence
*Community/Business Connections
*Respect for the Group Process
*Understand/Embrace
   Mission/Goals

Board Chairpersons should have as many of the following as possible:

Personal Characteristics

*Smart
*Energetic
*Business Sense
*Ability to Raise Funds
*Money to Give
*Chutzpah

*Status/Prominence/Well Respected
*Heart for Philanthropy/Cause
*Insightful
*Connections to Right People
*Willing to Cultivate Prospects
*Ability to Close on Asks

Professional Characteristics

*Skilled Meeting Facilitator
*Understand Board Responsibilities
*Can Differentiate Governance
  from Management Role
*Visible: Will Attend
  Events/Meetings
*Wise and Respected Counselor

*Strategic Thinker
*Cultivator
*Possess Good Judgment
*Committed to Do the Best
  for the Organization -
  Long/Short Term
 *Ability to Build Consensus

BOARD MEMBER POSITION DESCRIPTION

TITLE: Member (organization) Board of Directors

PURPOSE: To serve as a voting member of the body that has the authority and responsibility to develop policies, procedures, and regulations for the conduct of (organization's) mission and to actively participate in fundraising efforts.

TERMS: Three years (unless elected to fill an unexpired term of shorter duration). Subject to board term limits.

MEETING ATTENDANCE: Attend monthly board meetings. Attend committee meetings as scheduled. Attend special meetings when called. Board members who miss three consecutive meetings, unexcused, may be removed from the board by a majority of the members.

REPORTS TO: Board Chair

RESIGNATION: In writing to the Board Chair and Secretary.

GENERAL RESPONSIBILITIES:

1. Participate in establishing policies for administrating the programs and services that are in harmony with the mission of (organization).
2. Provide or help to secure funds for operating expenses through actively identifying potential donors of dollars or in-kind services and participating in various fundraising events.
3. Monitor the financial affairs on a responsible basis in accordance with established Board policies.
4. Ensure legal and ethical integrity/accountability are maintained.

SPECIFIC DUTIES:

1. Board member donations are critical in the fundraising process, as many funders require 100% of the board to support an organization before they will consider funding it themselves. As a result, we require board members to support the (organization) financially to the best of their ability, by:
   a. Annually making a personally meaningful gift;
   b. Selling tickets and sponsorships, and assisting with fundraising events whenever possible; and
   c. Garnering other financial or in-kind support from the community, individuals, and businesses.
2. Board member will support the (organization) with expertise when called upon.
3. Board member will advocate for and represent the (organization) in the most positive manner, including representing the (organization) at community events.
4. Attend board meetings regularly and on time.
   a. Become informed in advance on agenda items and supporting materials.
   b. Contribute knowledge and comments based on personal experience.
   c. Consider other points of view, make constructive suggestions, and help the board make decisions consistent with the agency's mission.
5. Attend meetings of any standing committees and ad hoc committees to which appointed.
6. Assume leadership when asked.
7. Hold in confidence all discussions and information given to the Board of Directors.
8. Be informed about (organization) programs and policies.
9. Attend as many (organization) events as possible, both fundraising and other types of events.
10. Become educated about the needs of the general community and citizens whose needs relate to the (organization's) mission.
11. Complete an annual Conflict of Interest statement.

12. Annually evaluate overall board performance as well as personal Board performance.

I have read and understand this board member position description.

Board Member Name:_____
Date:_____

QUESTIONS TO ASK BEFORE
JOINING A BOARD OF DIRECTORS

- ➤ What is the organization's mission? Am I interested and/or passionate about it?
- ➤ What are the current governance needs of the board and do I have the appropriate background to serve?
- ➤ Why am I being asked to be on this board? What does the organization anticipate I would contribute?
- ➤ Is there a list of board members, their titles, and affiliations?
- ➤ Is there a written "job" description for board members?
- ➤ Are board members expected to donate money? If so, how much?
- ➤ Is there an organizational chart?
- ➤ What is the time commitment expected of me for both board and committee work?
- ➤ What committees exist and do they have individual charters?
- ➤ What is the organization's financial condition? Can I see the most recent financial audit and IRS Form 990?
- ➤ Is there a current strategic plan for the organization? If so, am I interested/willing to help reach some of the goals?
- ➤ Does the board have Directors & Officers liability insurance?
- ➤ What are the major fundraising and program goals for the next 3 years?
- ➤ How am I expected to participate in fundraising for the organization?
- ➤ Does the organization have board orientation and board development activities?
- ➤ Can I go on a site-visit to see the program in action?
- ➤ Does the board do an annual self-evaluation?
- ➤ Do board members sign annual Conflict of Interest disclosure statements?

SHORT BOARD SELF-EVALUATION FORM

Using the following guide, please indicate your appraisal of each item.
1 = Never a problem   **2 = Seldom a problem**
3 = Increasingly a problem   **4 = Now a definite hindrance**

Practical Considerations
1   2   3   4

Are you able to meet the time commitments of _____?
☐   ☐   ☐   ☐

Are you able to attend regularly scheduled meetings?
☐   ☐   ☐   ☐

Do you foresee conflicts between responsibilities to your family
☐   ☐   ☐   ☐
and the demands of this position?

Is your schedule flexible enough for you to make emergency
☐   ☐   ☐   ☐
board and committee meetings?

Does this position conflict with your job or other commitments?
☐   ☐   ☐   ☐

Clarifying remarks:

_____

Individual Considerations
1   2   3   4

Do you have a high level of commitment and interest in _____?
☐   ☐   ☐   ☐

Are you able to discuss controversial topics effectively?
☐   ☐   ☐   ☐

Do you find yourself tense and hostile during candid exchanges of opinion?

❑   ❑   ❑   ❑

Do you work easily with other board members and the director?

❑   ❑   ❑   ❑

Are you able to keep an open mind on issues?

❑   ❑   ❑   ❑

Are you a willing and enthusiastic promoter for _____?

❑   ❑   ❑   ❑

Do you make an annual financial gift to _____?

❑   ❑   ❑   ❑

❑   In light of the above, I would like to be considered for another term of ____ years.

❑   In light of the above, I can no longer make the commitment to serve on the board.

_____   _____

Signature   Date

BOARD MEETING ASSESSMENT SURVEY

We recommend periodically using a board meeting assessment survey to gather members' thoughts about the effectiveness of a meeting. This tool can identify specific issues that may need to be addressed, thus helping to keep board members engaged and committed to their volunteer service.

Board Meeting Date _____

WHAT IS YOUR ROLE ON THE BOARD?

____Member   ____Officer
____Emeritus   ____Ex Officio

DID YOU FEEL THE MEETING AGENDA WAS SUFFICIENT FOR THE ORGANIZATION'S BUSINESS?

____Yes   ____No
____Too much on the agenda to adequately be addressed in the time allowed
Other:

_____

_____

WERE YOU ABLE TO REVIEW THE MEETING MATERIALS BEFORE THE MEETING?

____Yes   ____No
If no, why not?

_____

_____

DID YOU COME TO THE BOARD MEETING WITH A SPECIFIC ISSUE OR CONCERN YOU WANTED ADDRESSED?

____Yes   ____No

If yes, please explain: -

_____

_____

IF YES, WAS THIS ADDRESSED TO YOUR SATISFACTION?

____Yes   ____No

Please explain:

_____

_____

DID YOU PARTICIPATE IN THE DISCUSSION DURING THE MEETING?

____Yes   ____No

If no, why not?

_____

_____

DO YOU FEEL THE MEETING WAS A GOOD USE OF YOUR TIME?

____Yes   ____No

If no, why not?

_____

_____

WHAT DID YOU FIND MOST MEANINGFUL DURING THE MEETING?

(check all that apply)

____Information provided by staff   ____Discussion
____New business   ____Finance information
____Networking opportunities   ____Committee Reports

Other:

_____

ARE YOU SATISFIED WITH THE PROCESS USED TO MAKE DECISIONS AND HOW THE MEETING WAS CONDUCTED?

_____An excellent meeting   _____ A good meeting
_____A frustrating meeting   _____Not feeling good about it
Please
explain:_____

_____

DO YOU HAVE ANY SUGGESTIONS FOR CHANGES YOU WOULD LIKE TO SEE MADE IN HOW BOARD MEETINGS ARE CONDUCTED?

_____Yes   _____No
If yes, please explain:

_____

_____

BOARD MEMBER REMOVAL PROCEDURE

We recommend including in the organization's by-laws a section that addresses removal of a board member, and that a policy describing the process be adopted by the board. The following are two different examples of by-laws language which have been employed by other nonprofits.

Example 1: Any director may be removed from office, without assigning any cause, by the vote of two-thirds of the entire board at any meeting of the Board.

Example 2: The Board of Directors may, by at least a two-thirds (2/3) majority vote of all voting directors then in office, remove any director, including active voting directors or Directors Emeritus, for cause, from the Board of Directors and immediately declare vacant such director's slot on the Board of Directors. For purposes hereof, "cause" shall include: (i) conviction of a felony or other crime of moral turpitude; (ii) unprofessional or disruptive conduct; (iii) failure to comply with the organization's policies; (iv) continued physical, mental or emotional impairment precluding effective service on the Board of Directors; (v) breach of fiduciary duties to the organization; and (vi) any other acts or omissions not in the best interests of the organization.

Suggested board member removal procedure wording to be adopted by the board:

The by-laws of the (organization), revised and adopted on (date), provide for the removal of a board member under certain circumstances. It is recognized that this is a step that should be taken as a last resort after other means have been attempted to deal with the situation and have not worked. The following procedure is adopted to ensure that such removal is done in as fair and organized manner as possible.

Step 1: The Executive Committee will meet to discuss the situation. If the Executive Committee determines that the situation is beyond correction with the member in question, Step 2 will be employed.

Step 2: The Board Chair will meet with the member in question and ask the member to willingly resign.

Step 3: If the member resigns, that member will write a letter of resignation to the Board Chair; this letter will be presented to the board at its next regularly scheduled meeting. The letter will then be placed in the organization's file on board activity. The process and procedure will then be considered completed.

Step 4: If the member does not willingly resign, the matter will be brought to the board for action of removal either at its next regularly scheduled meeting or at a special meeting called at the discretion of the Board Chair. Action for removal will be considered approved with the "YES" vote of a majority of those board members present at the meeting voting "YES."

CONFLICT OF INTEREST POLICY

PURPOSE:

The purpose of this policy is to protect the interest of (organization) and any of its affiliates (collectively, the "Corporation") when it is contemplating entering into a transaction or arrangement that might benefit the private interest of a director, officer, member of a committee or employee. This policy is intended to supplement, but not replace, any applicable state laws governing conflicts of interest.

POLICY:

1. Identification of Conflict or Potential Conflict of Interest.

A conflict or potential conflict of interest exists in:

(a)   any transaction or arrangement between the Corporation and a director, officer or member of a committee;

(b)   any transaction or arrangement between the Corporation and any entity or individual (1) in which or with which a director, officer or committee member is an officer or director or has a financial interest, or (2) in which or with which any director, officer or committee member otherwise has any conflict of interest; and

(c)   any transaction or arrangement in which a director, officer or committee member otherwise has a financial interest.

A director, officer or committee member has a "financial interest" if such person, directly or indirectly, whether through business, investment or family has a present or potential ownership or investment interest or compensation arrangement in or with an entity or individual with which the Corporation has or may have a transaction or arrangement. Compensation includes direct and indirect remuneration as well as gifts and favors that are substantial in nature.

Any director, officer or committee member who has a conflict or potential conflict of interest with respect to any transaction or arrangement is hereinafter referred to as an "interested person."

2. Disclosure of Conflict or Potential Conflict of Interest.

In connection with any transaction or arrangement presented or to be presented to the Board of Directors of the Corporation (or committee thereof), each interested person is required to make a prompt, full and frank disclosure of the material facts relating to the conflict or potential conflict to the Board of Directors (or committee).

3. Determination of Conflict of Interest.

After disclosure of the conflict or potential conflict of interest, including the relevant financial interest, and all material facts and after any discussion with the interested person, it shall be the obligation of the Board of Directors (or committee, as applicable), without the participation of the interested person and, where appropriate, outside such person's presence, to make a determination whether a conflict of interest exists.

4. Interested Person's Participation.

If a conflict of interest is determined to exist, the interested person may make a presentation at the board or committee meeting, as appropriate, but after such presentation, he/she shall leave the meeting during the discussion of, and the vote on, the transaction or arrangement that results in the conflict of interest. The interested person shall not vote on and shall not use any personal influence with respect to the vote on such transaction or arrangement. Notwithstanding the foregoing, if the conflict of interest arises in connection with a proposed grant by the Corporation to a grantee organization that qualifies as a Section 501(c)(3) organization under the Internal Revenue Code ("Code") and that is a public charity and not a private foundation under the Code (a "Qualified Grantee"), and if the conflict of interest is due solely to the fact that a director of the Corporation is also serving as a volunteer director of the Qualified Grantee, the interested director shall not be required to leave the meeting during the discussion of, and vote on, the proposed grant, but shall not vote on and shall not use any personal influence with respect to the vote on such grant.

5. Action on the Transaction or Arrangement.

After exercising due diligence, the board or committee, as appropriate, shall determine whether the Corporation can obtain a more advantageous transaction or arrangement with reasonable efforts from a person or entity that would not give rise to a conflict of interest. The decision to enter into a transaction or arrangement involving an interested person requires at a minimum a majority vote of the non-interested directors (or committee members) present. Those directors (or committee members) may approve the transaction or arrangement only after making the determination that: (a) the Corporation could not have obtained a more advantageous transaction or arrangement with reasonable efforts from a person or entity that would not give rise to a conflict of interest; and (b) the transaction or arrangement is in the Corporation's best interest and for the Corporation's benefit and is fair and reasonable to the Corporation. The non-interested directors (or committee members) may if appropriate appoint a non-interested person or committee to investigate alternatives to the proposed transaction or arrangement.

6. Minutes.
The minutes of the board (or committee) meeting shall include the name of the person who disclosed a conflict or potential conflict of interest or was otherwise found to have a conflict of interest, the nature of the conflict and underlying financial interest and whether the board (or committee) determined that there was a conflict of interest. In addition, the minutes shall identify those persons who were present for discussions and votes relating to the transaction or arrangement, shall summarize the contents of these discussions, including any alternatives to the proposed transaction or arrangement which were discussed, and shall record the vote.

7. Violations of the Conflicts or Interest Policy.

(a)   If the board (or committee) has reasonable cause to believe that a director, officer or committee member has failed to disclose actual or possible conflicts of interest, it shall inform such person of the basis for such belief and afford such person an opportunity to explain the alleged failure to disclose.

(b)   If, after hearing the response of the person and making such further investigation as may be warranted in the circumstances, the board (or committee) determines that the person has in fact failed to disclose an actual or possible conflict of interest, it shall take appropriate disciplinary and corrective action.

8. Annual Statements.

Each director, officer and committee member shall annually sign a statement which affirms that such person:

(a)   has received a copy of the conflicts of interest policy;

(b)   has read and understands the policy;

(c)   has agreed to comply with the policy; and

(d)   understands that the Corporation is a charitable organization and that in order to maintain its federal tax exemption, it must engage primarily in activities which accomplish one or more of its tax-exempt purposes.

9. Periodic Reviews.

To ensure that the Corporation operates in a manner consistent with its charitable purposes and that it does not engage in activities that could jeopardize its status as an organization exempt from federal income tax, periodic reviews shall he conducted. The periodic reviews shall, at a minimum, include the following subjects:

(a)   Whether compensation arrangements and benefits are reasonable and are the result of arm's-length bargaining;

(b)   Whether financial arrangements conform to written policies, are properly recorded, reflect reasonable payments for goods and services, further the Corporation's charitable purposes and do not result in inurement or impermissible private benefit or in impermissible excess benefits under Section 4958 of the Code; and

(c)   Whether agreements entered into further the Corporation's charitable purposes and do not result in inurement or impermissible private benefit or in impermissible excess benefits under Section 4958 of the Code.

In conducting periodic reviews, the Corporation may, but need not, use outside advisors. If outside experts are used, their use shall not relieve the Board of its responsibilities for ensuring that periodic reviews are conducted.

10. Applicability to Designated Employees.

A conflict or potential conflict of interest may also exist in:

(a)   any transaction or arrangement between the Corporation and an employee,

(b)   any transaction or arrangement between the Corporation and any entity or individual (1) in which or with which an employee is an officer or director or has a financial interest, or (2) in which or with which any employee otherwise has any conflict of interest; and

(c)   any transaction or arrangement in which an employee otherwise has a financial interest.

Accordingly, an employee may not enter into a transaction or arrangement with an outside party, either directly or indirectly, which will result in personal benefit to such employee at the expense of the Corporation without the knowledge and consent of the Corporation.

An employee who is involved in any business or organization that conducts business with, or is in direct competition with, the Corporation shall disclose such interest to the Corporation and shall not participate in any decisions concerning transactions with such business or organization. If during the regular course of business a conflict of interest arises between the role of the employee as employee of the Corporation and the role of the employee with respect to another business or organization, the conflict shall be immediately disclosed to the Corporation and the employee shall not take any action which might compromise the interests of the Corporation.

It shall be the obligation of the President of the Corporation, or his/her designee, to make a determination whether a conflict of interest exists, except as to matters involving the President as to which it shall be the obligation of the Board Chair to make the applicable determination.

Individuals who violate this policy are, among other things, subject to disciplinary action, including loss of employment.

DATE APPROVED: _____

ANNUAL STATEMENT AND DISCLOSURE

CONCERNING CONFLICT OF INTEREST

NAME: _____

1. Background.

Service on the Board of Directors of the Corporation or an affiliate (collectively the "Corporation") or on a committee of the board or as an officer of the Corporation carries with it a duty of loyalty to the goals, programs, charitable mission and business interests of the Corporation and requires good faith and fair dealing with regard to the Corporation. Among other things, personal involvement with any outside entity or individual which results in conduct of the type described below is in conflict with this responsibility:

(a)   Competing against the Corporation or depriving the Corporation of any business opportunity, in either case without the knowledge and consent of the Corporation;

(b)   Realizing personal financial gain from a transaction with the Corporation at the expense of the Corporation without the knowledge and consent of the Corporation; and

(c)   Conduct which has the potential to adversely impact the Corporation.

Accordingly, no board member, committee member or officer may enter into any transaction or arrangement with any outside party, either directly or indirectly, which will result in personal benefit to such individual at the expense of the Corporation without the knowledge and consent of the Corporation or affiliate, as applicable. Further, a board member, committee member, or officer who is involved, directly or indirectly, in any business or organization that conducts business with the Corporation shall disclose such interest to the Corporation and shall not participate in any decisions concerning transactions with such business or organization. Individuals who violate this policy are, among other things, subject to loss of their appointment to the board or applicable committee or their appointment as an officer.

2. Affirmations Regarding the Conflicts Policy.

This is to affirm that the undersigned:

(a)   has received a copy of the conflicts of interest policy of the Corporation;

(b)   has read and understands the policy;

(c)   agrees to comply with the policy; and

(d)   understands that the Corporation is a charitable organization and that in order to maintain its federal tax exemption, it must engage primarily in activities which accomplish one or more of its tax exempt purposes.

3. Disclosures.

[ ]   I hereby warrant that I am not aware of any conflict of interest or potential conflict of interest concerning the business and affairs of the Corporation and my position as director, officer or committee member of the Corporation.

[ ]   I hereby disclose the following conflict of interest or possible conflict of interest, including without limitation my involvement in any business or organization that conducts business with, or is in direct competition with, the Corporation:

4. Obligation to Update.

I agree to update this Statement in writing if there are any changes in the information contained herein, including without limitation immediately declaring any conflict or possible conflict of interest which arises in the regular course of business.

Signature of Individual:_____

Date: _____

POLICY CONCERNING CONFLICT OF INTEREST

INVOLVING EMPLOYEES

NAME: _____

1. <u>Background</u>.

Employment by the Corporation carries with it the obligation of loyalty and fidelity to the goals, programs, charitable mission, and business interests of the Corporation. Among other things, personal involvement with any outside entity or individual which results in conduct of the type described below is in conflict with this responsibility:

(a)   Competing against the Corporation or an affiliate or depriving the Corporation or an affiliate of any business opportunity, in either case without the knowledge and consent of the Corporation or affiliate, as applicable;

(b)   Realizing personal financial gain from a transaction with the Corporation or an affiliate at the expense of the Corporation or affiliate without the knowledge and consent of the Corporation or affiliate, as applicable; and

(c)   Conduct which has the potential to adversely impact the Corporation or an affiliate.

Accordingly, an employee may not enter into a transaction or arrangement with an outside party, either directly or indirectly, which will result in personal benefit to the such employee at the expense of the Corporation or an affiliate without the knowledge and consent of the Corporation or affiliate, as applicable. Individuals who violate this policy are, among other things, subject to disciplinary action, including loss of employment.

2. <u>Conflicts of Interest</u>.

An employee who is involved, directly or indirectly, in any business or organization that conducts business with the Corporation or its affiliates shall disclose such interest to the Corporation and shall not participate in any decisions concerning transactions with such business or organization. If during the regular course of business a conflict of interest arises between the role of the employee as employee of the Corporation and the role of the employee with respect to another business or organization, the conflict shall be immediately disclosed to the Corporation and the employee shall not take any action which might compromise the interests of the Corporation or its affiliates. Individuals who violate this policy are, among other things, subject to disciplinary action, including loss of employment.

3. Disclosures.

Employees shall warrant that they are not aware of any conflict of interest or potential conflict of interest concerning the business and affairs of the Corporation and their employment with the Corporation. Employees shall disclose any conflict of interest or possible conflict of interest, including without limitation any involvement in any business or organization that conducts business with the Corporation or any of its affiliates that may arise in the regular course of business.

4. Tax-exempt Mission.

Employees must understand that the Corporation is a charitable organization and that in order to maintain its federal tax exemption, it must engage primarily in activities which accomplish one or more of its tax-exempt purposes.

5. Acknowledgment and Agreement.

The undersigned acknowledges that he/she has read and understands this policy, has been given an opportunity to ask questions concerning the policy, and agrees to be bound by the policy.

Signature of Individual:
_____ Date: _____

WHISTLEBLOWER POLICY

General

The (organization's) Code of Ethics and Conduct requires directors, officers, and employees to observe high standards of business and personal ethics in the conduct of their duties and responsibilities. As employees and representatives of the (organization), we must practice honesty and integrity in fulfilling our responsibilities and comply with all applicable laws and regulations.

Reporting Responsibility

It is the responsibility of all directors, officers, and employees to comply with the Code and to report violations or suspected violations in accordance with this Whistleblower Policy.

No Retaliation

No director, officer, or employee who in good faith reports a violation of the Code shall suffer harassment, retaliation, or adverse employment consequence. An employee who retaliates against someone who has reported a violation in good faith is subject to discipline up to and including termination of employment. This Whistleblower Policy is intended to encourage and enable employees and others to raise serious concerns within the (organization) prior to seeking resolution outside the (organization).

Reporting Violations

The Code addresses the (organization's) open door policy and suggests that employees share their questions, concerns, suggestions, or complaints with someone who can address them properly. In most cases, an employee's supervisor is in the best position to address an area of concern. However, if an employee is not comfortable speaking with their supervisor or they are not satisfied with their supervisor's response, he/she is encouraged to speak with the Chair of the (organization's) Board of Directors. Supervisors and managers are required to report suspected violations of the Code of Ethics and Conduct to the (organization's) Compliance Officer, who has specific and exclusive responsibility to investigate all reported violations. For suspected fraud, or when they are not satisfied or are uncomfortable with following the (organization's) open door policy, individuals should contact the (organization's) Compliance Officer directly.

Compliance Officer

The (organization's) Compliance Officer is the Chair of the Executive Committee. The (organization's) Compliance Officer is responsible for investigating and resolving all reported complaints and allegations concerning violations of the Code and, at his/her discretion, shall advise the (organization's) Executive Director and or the Executive Committee. The Compliance Officer has direct access to the Executive Committee of the Board of Directors and is required to report to the Executive Committee as least annually on compliance activity.

Accounting and Auditing Matters

The Executive Committee of the Board of Directors shall address all reported concerns or complaints regarding corporate accounting practices, internal controls, or auditing. The Compliance Officer shall immediately notify the Executive Committee of any such complaint and work with the committee until the matter is resolved.

Acting in Good Faith

Anyone filing a complaint concerning a violation or suspected violation of the Code must be acting in good faith and have reasonable grounds for believing the information disclosed indicates a violation of the Code. Any allegations that prove not to be substantiated and which prove to have been made maliciously or knowingly to be false will be viewed as a serious disciplinary offense.

Confidentiality

Violations or suspected violations may be submitted on a confidential basis by the complainant or may be submitted anonymously. Reports of violations or suspected violations will be kept confidential to the extent possible, consistent with the need to conduct an adequate investigation.

Handling of Reported Violations
The Compliance Officer will notify the sender and acknowledge receipt of the reported violation or suspected violation within five business days. All reports will be investigated promptly and appropriate corrective action will be taken if warranted by the investigation.

This policy has been unanimously adopted by the Board of Directors.

_____   _____

Board Chair   Date

DOCUMENT DESTRUCTION/RETENTION POLICY

Purpose

The Sarbanes-Oxley Act addresses the destruction of business records and documents and turns intentional document destruction into a process that must be carefully monitored.

Nonprofit organizations should have a written, mandatory document retention and periodic destruction policy. Policies such as this will eliminate accidental or innocent destruction. In addition, it is important for administrative personnel to know the length of time that records should be retained to be in compliance.

The document destruction/retention policy table includes the following parameters:

Type of Document	Minimum Requirement
Accounts payable ledgers and schedules	7 years
Audit reports	Permanently
Bank reconciliations	2 years
Bank statements	3 years
Checks (for important payments and purchases)	Permanently
Contracts, mortgages, notes and leases (expired)	7 years
Contracts (still in effect)	Permanently
Correspondence (general)	2 years
Correspondence (legal and important mattes)	Permanently
Correspondence (with customers and vendors)	2 years
Deeds, mortgages, and bill of sale	Permanently
Depreciation schedules	Permanently
Duplicate deposit slips	2 years
Employment applications	3 years

Expense analyses/expense distribution schedules	7 years
Year-end financial statements	Permanently
Insurance policies (expired)	3 years
Insurance records, current accident reports, claims, policies, etc.	Permanently
Internal audit reports	3 years
Inventories of products, materials, and supplies	7 years
Invoices (to customers; from vendors)	7 years
Minute books, by-laws, and charter	Permanently
Patents and related papers	Permanently
Payroll records and summaries	7 years
Personnel files (terminated employees)	7 years
Retirement and pension records	Permanently
Tax returns and worksheets	Permanently
Time sheets	7 years
Trademark registrations and copyrights	Permanently
Withholding tax statements	7 years

(Organization's) staff are responsible for reviewing documents under the following categories: grants, programs, and administration.

All documents on the (organization's) server are backed up on the cloud.

This policy has been unanimously adopted by the Board of Directors.

_____   _____

Board Chair   Date

CREATING AN EMERGENCY PLAN

Developing an emergency plan includes five key components:

➢ People,

➢ Workspace,

➢ Technology, data, and records,

➢ Suppliers and partners, and

➢ Communication and outreach.

Identify the specific requirements for the organization and determine the recovery time goals for each component. There may be different priorities depending on the nature of the organization. All of the items below are not applicable to all nonprofits; address only the ones that apply.

PEOPLE

➢ Identify the events most likely to occur that would prevent people from working. Prioritize your planning to recover from the most likely events.

➢ Identify all people essential to the operation of your organization, including staff, board members, volunteers, suppliers, contractors, etc.

➢ Obtain alternate contact information for all essential people.

➢ Determine if the essential people can get to an alternate location without assistance. Do they have cars or are they dependent on rides or public transportation utilizing specific routes that may be compromised in an emergency?

- ➤ Determine if any of the essential people have special needs that need to be factored into the planning.

- ➤ What are the job skills essential for the organization's survival?
  - ✓ How many people have those skills? Develop cross training or job-sharing protocols if the skills are limited to one or two people.
  - ✓ What shifts do they work?
  - ✓ Are they reliable? Do any have family responsibilities that would limit their availability in an emergency?

- ➤ Determine the minimum number of people required to run the organization.
  - ✓ In an emergency, what roles are essential vs. those that could be suspended?
  - ✓ Determine the minimum number of essential people.
  - ✓ Are enough people available to provide essential skills on each shift?

- ➤ Are essential procedures documented so others could follow them? Ensure that multiple people understand and can follow procedures, not just the person who wrote them.

WORKSPACE

- ➤ Identify the most likely events that would prevent access to the workspace. Prioritize planning to recover from the most likely events.

- ➤ Identify characteristics of the workspace that are essential to run the organization, such as: location, parking, public transportation, ramps, elevators, generated power, kitchen facilities, etc.

- ➤ What contents of the workspace (tools, computers, paper records/files, supplies, etc.) are absolutely essential to run the organization?

- Identify possible alternative workspaces, such as: hotels, fire halls or fire stations, banquet facilities, vacant office space, or a warehouse.

- Network with a local commercial realtor who might be able to help identify alternative office space in an emergency.

- Develop reciprocal relationships with other similar organizations.

TECHNOLOGY, DATA, RECORDS

- Identify the events most likely to prevent access to essential records and data. Prioritize planning to recover from the most likely events.

- Determine the information that is essential to run the organization.
    - Is the information protected adequately based on its level of importance?
    - Are sufficient cyber security programs in place?
    - Is the information in paper or digital form?

- Is there more than one copy or backup of the essential information? Are the copies stored off-site and/or cloud-based?

- Is all information stored to maintain confidentiality?

- Can the information be accessed remotely?

- Determine the essential technology needed to access the information: portable laptops, remote access to a server, etc. Are staff trained in accessing the information remotely?

- Is backup technology available, such as spare up-to-date computers loaded with appropriate software that can be provided to staff.

> Does the organization contract with an IT professional/company that will be available in an emergency? If not, establish that relationship.

SUPPLIERS AND PARTNERS

> Identify the events most likely to disrupt your suppliers or prevent access to your essential partners. Prioritize planning to recover from the most likely events.

> Identify external partners that are essential to run the nonprofit, such as a parent organization, government entities, and/or regulatory organizations.

> Identify suppliers that are essential to run the nonprofit, such as suppliers of medications, supplies, equipment rentals, delivery organizations, and/or contracted services.

> Determine how resilient the essential suppliers and partners are.
>> ✓ Do they have emergency plans?
>> ✓ Can they continue to function and provide services in an emergency?

> Obtain alternate contact information for essential suppliers and partners, such as after-hours phone numbers, cell phone numbers, personal e-mail addresses, etc.

> Identify alternate suppliers and consider using them occasionally to develop relationships.

COMMUNICATION AND OUTREACH

Develop a Contact List

> Identify the people and organizations to be called in an emergency, such as staff, board members, volunteers, suppliers, partners,

public agencies, clients, customers, emergency responders, authorities, etc.

➤ Identify how much time would be needed to call them and gather the necessary contact information, such as name, cell, work and home phone numbers, e-mail addresses, key skills and roles in an emergency, and names and contact information for alternates.

➤ Determine how the time of day or the nature of the emergency would affect who is contacted.

Develop the Message

➤ Develop a generic message that can be used as a basis for specific emergencies, ensuring the factual information about your nonprofit is accurate.

➤ Designate a spokesperson to represent the organization in a crisis and an alternate.

Develop Communication Tools

➤ Ensure a variety of communication tools are in place, such as:
   ✓ An up-to-date phone tree
   ✓ Emergency notification system: cell phones, pagers
   ✓ E-mail and text-capable devices
   ✓ Internet
   ✓ Social Media

EQUAL EMPLOYMENT/VOLUNTEER OPPORTUNITY

NON-DISCRIMINATION POLICY

In order to provide equal employment and advancement opportunities to all individuals, employment decisions at (organization) will be based on merit, qualifications, and abilities. (Organization) does not discriminate in employment/volunteer opportunities or practices on the basis of race, color, religion, sex, national origin, age, disability, or any other characteristic protected by law.

We will make reasonable accommodations for qualified individuals with known disabilities unless doing so would result in an undue hardship for the organization. This policy covers all aspects of employment/ volunteering, including selection, job assignment, compensation, discipline, termination, and access to benefits and training.

If you have a question or concern about any type of discrimination in the workplace, you are encouraged to bring the issue to the attention of the Executive Director. At (organization), individuals can be assured that they can raise concerns and make reports without fear of reprisal. Further, anyone found to be engaging in any type of unlawful discrimination will be subject to disciplinary action, up to and including termination of employment.

Furthermore, it is the policy of (organization) that services will be provided to all individuals who are eligible without discrimination on the basis of HIV infection, race, creed, color, age, sex, gender, sexual orientation, religion, ancestry, national origin, physical or mental handicap (including substance abuse), immigration status, political affiliation or belief.

This policy has been adopted unanimously by the full Board of Directors.

_____   _____
Board Chair   Date

HARASSMENT POLICY

(Organization) is committed to providing a work environment that is free from all forms of discrimination and conduct that can be considered harassing, coercive, or disruptive, including sexual harassment. Actions, words, jokes, or comments based on an individual's sex, race, color, national origin, age, religion, disability, sexual orientation, or any other legally protected characteristic will not be tolerated. Such conduct will result in disciplinary action up to and including dismissal of an employee/volunteer/board/committee member who harasses others.

Sexual harassment is defined as unwanted sexual advances, or visual, verbal, or physical conduct of a sexual nature. This definition includes many forms of offensive behavior and includes gender-based harassment of a person of the same sex as the harasser.

The following is a partial list of sexual harassment examples:

- Unwanted sexual advances.
- Offering employment benefits in exchange for sexual favors.
- Making or threatening reprisals after a negative response to sexual advances.
- Visual conduct that includes leering, making sexual gestures, or displaying of sexually suggestive objects or pictures, cartoons, or posters, digital or printed.
- Verbal conduct that includes using derogatory comments, epithets, slurs, or jokes.
- Verbal sexual advances or propositions.
- Verbal abuse of a sexual nature, graphic verbal commentaries about an individual's body, sexually degrading words used to describe an individual, suggestive or obscene letters, notes, or invitations.
- Physical conduct that includes touching, assaulting, impeding or blocking movements.

Unwelcome sexual advances (either verbal or physical), requests for sexual favors, and other verbal or physical conduct of a sexual nature constitute sexual harassment when: (1) submission to such conduct is made either explicitly or implicitly a term or condition of employment;

(2) submission or rejection of the conduct is used as a basis for making employment decisions; or (3) the conduct has the purpose or effect of interfering with work performance or creating an intimidating, hostile, or offensive work environment.

If you experience or witness sexual or other unlawful harassment in the workplace, report it immediately to the Executive Director. You can raise concerns and make reports without fear of reprisal or retaliation.

All allegations of sexual harassment or other unlawful forms of harassment will be quickly and discreetly investigated. To the extent possible, your confidentiality and that of any witnesses and the alleged harasser will be protected against unnecessary disclosure. When the investigation is completed, you will be informed of the outcome of the investigation.

When the Executive Director becomes aware of possible sexual or other unlawful harassment, he/she must immediately advise the Board Chair so it can be investigated in a timely and confidential manner. Any employee/volunteer/board/committee member engaging in sexual or other unlawful harassment will be subject to disciplinary action, up to and including termination of employment/volunteer position/membership.

DONOR INFORMATION POLICY

All information about donors and prospective donors (names, demographic data, giving history, personal and professional information, etc.) shall be held confidential by all staff and volunteers.

(Organization's) mailing lists shall not be sold, rented, loaned, or shared with any other organization or business under any circumstances, except with the express permission of the Executive Director and the Chair of the Board of Directors.

CEO SUCCESSION PLANNING PROCEDURE

It is understood that the (organization) and its employees are managed by the President/CEO. While maintaining the separation of power/authority, all staff of (organization) should maintain familiarity and be able to carry out the core functions of the organization during a short-term absence of the President/CEO.

Procedure for a Short-Term Vacancy

A short-term vacancy is one in which the President/CEO is anticipated to be out no more than 90 days and is expected to return to the leadership role. The Board of Directors may appoint an Acting/Interim President/CEO.

The board chair shall convene a meeting of the Executive Committee as soon as possible to review the circumstances surrounding the absence and determine if an Acting/Interim President/CEO is needed to assure the continued smooth operation of the (organization). If an Acting/Interim President/CEO is needed, it will be the Executive Committee's responsibility to recommend a candidate to the full board. This candidate may be an employee of the organization or an independent contractor who has the proper credentials and qualifications. Whether it is an existing employee or contractor, compensation will be based on an amount to be agreed upon.

The Acting/Interim President/CEO shall have the full authority for decision making and independent action as the regular President/CEO except for duties related to banking and investments. These will be performed by the remaining regular signatories of the (organization). The board chair will also be responsible for developing a message to appropriate internal and external stakeholders communicating the temporary change for use on the website and in other publications.

Procedure for a Permanent Vacancy

In the event of an unplanned or planned permanent departure of the President/CEO, the staff will serve to fulfill the daily requirements of operations while the Board of Directors commences the process for recruitment of a new President/CEO.

Upon learning of the vacancy of the President/CEO the Chairperson shall notify the Board of Directors. A special meeting may be called, depending on the dates and times for the regularly scheduled board meeting, for the purpose of initiating the process of filling the vacancy. The board chair will develop a communication vehicle to community stakeholders about the vacancy.

The process will include the following:

1. The board shall reaffirm the (organization's) mission, vision, and guiding principles. The board will also confirm the necessary qualifications based on these needs. The most recent job description of the President/CEO shall be used as a reference.

2. An Ad Hoc Search Committee will be appointed by the Executive Committee. This committee will consist of no fewer than three but no more than five members of the board. The skills and abilities of the committee members should include those best suited to personnel recruitment. This committee will take responsibility for all procedures, including the development of the following:

> - A new job description, if necessary,
> - A written document posting the job in appropriate publications, if necessary,
> - Drafting an employment agreement,
> - Engaging a search firm, if necessary,
> - Questions to be posed to candidates during the interview, and
> - Development of a salary range based upon recent salary surveys of comparable organizations.

3. The committee will then gather the names and resumes of candidates for the position to determine a pool of viable candidates. The committee will interview a selected number of the best candidates and recommend up to four candidates for a full board review. If desired and appropriate, interviews between finalists and key staff may also be conducted.

4. The candidates will be invited to meet the entire board at a special meeting. After the candidates meet with the board, the committee will contact references, and make a final recommendation to the entire board.

5. The full board will vote for the formal approval of hiring the selected candidate.

Conditions of Employment and Orientation

A letter of intent and conditions of employment should be provided including terms of employment, salary, insurance, and details about any other benefits.

When the new President/CEO is selected and approved, the Executive Committee will secure the acknowledgement from that individual that he/she is in complete and full agreement with the terms of employment and the goals of (organization). The Governance Committee will provide a complete orientation program for the new President/CEO, including an overview of the history of the (organization), its programs, priorities, goals, and objectives. The board will authorize a formal announcement to all internal and community stakeholders about the selection of the new President/CEO.

If necessary, appropriate, and agreed to, the former President/CEO may be retained, at a contractual compensation rate to be determined, for a defined period of time not to exceed 180 days, to assist with the transition.

GRANT REQUEST FORM

This form collects two main categories of information:
- ➤ The Background Information section provides just what the term means – contact, grant usage, and request authorization information for clarity and follow-up reasons, if necessary.
- ➤ The Governance and Financial Health sections relate to two commonly accepted indicators of strength for a nonprofit organization.

Within the Governance category, the funder is testing for three issues:
- ➤ the agency's demographic diversity,
- ➤ how active the board is, and
- ➤ how organized the agency is from a best practices standpoint.

The Fiscal Health category contains 13 financial health ratios which give information and insight into the financial health or weakness of the agency.

BACKGROUND INFORMATION

Request Date:_____   Employer I.D. Number:_____

Federal Tax Determination Date: _____

Fed. Tax Exemption Classification: _____

Check Public Charity Status: Section 509(a)(1) _____ Section 509(a)(2) _____

    Section 509(a)(3) _____

If a Section 509(a)(3) Public Charity, please check type:

Type I ___ Type II ____Type III - Functionally Integrated ___

    Type III ___ Other: _____

Name of Organization: _____

Complete Street Address or PO Box -

_____

City/State/ZIP: _____

School District: _____

Telephone No.: _____ Fax No.: _____

Chief Staff Member: _____ Title: _____

Contact Person: _____ Title: _____

Email Address:_____

Web Address:_____

Mission of the Organization: _____

_____

Municipality in which activities are to be conducted: _

_____

Proposed use of grant funds: [*check all that apply*]

*General Operating Support _____ *Program _____ *Technology_____

*Capital Needs _____ *Capacity-Building _____ *Endowment _____

*Other: _____

Specific Description of Proposed Use of Grant Funds:

_____

_____

_____

Please indicate whether there has been any change in the organization's purpose, character, or method of operation since the issuance of its IRS tax ruling:
YES _____ NO _____

If acting as fiduciary agent for another party/organization, please attach a 1-page letter of explanation/support. (Define relationship between agencies; express commitment to the project/programs success)

Amount Requested $ _____

This grant request is being submitted with the knowledge and authorization of the Board of Directors.

Name:_____ Board President/Chair

Signature:_____ Date:_____

GOVERNANCE INFORMATION:

Number on your Board: _____

Number on Board in following demographic distributions:

Age: Under 30 _____ 30-44 _____ 45-59 _____ 60 and over _____

Race: Caucasian _____   African-American _____

           Latino-American _____   Asian-American _____

           Other _____

Gender: Male _____   Female _____

Background: Finance/Accounting _____   Marketing/PR/Adv _____

           Management (general) _____   Law _____

           Human Resources _____   Fundraising _____

           Program _____   Consumer _____

           Other (specify) _____

Check the Standing Board Committees that exist:

    Executive ____   Personnel ____   Fundraising ____   Program ____

    Governance ____   Finance ____   Audit ____

    Other (specify) _____

Does each Board Member serve on a committee: YES _____   NO _____

The Board of Directors generally meets _____ times a year

Board Committees generally meet _____ times per year

Number of Board Members who support your organization by:

    Donating money _____ Providing in-kind gifts/services _____
    Cultivating fundraising contacts _____
    Other (specify) _____

Has your Board adopted a:

Mission Statement: YES _____ NO _____ if "yes", when developed? _____
Vision Statement: YES _____ NO _____ if "yes", when developed? _____
Values Statement: YES _____ NO _____ if "yes", when developed? _____
Conflict of Interest Policy YES ____ NO ____ if "yes", when developed? _____
Whistle-Blower Policy YES_____ NO_____ if "yes", when developed? _____
Document Retention/Destruction Policy YES _____ NO _____
    if "yes", when developed? _____

Disaster Recovery Policy YES___ NO __ if "yes", when developed? _____
Personnel Policie   YES   NO   if "yes", when developed? _____
Strategic Plan: YES _____ NO _____ if "yes", when developed? _____
    Does the Board actively review the plan? YES ____ NO ____
    If YES, how often? _____

VOLUNTEER PARTICIPATION IN YOUR ORGANIZATION:

Estimated number of volunteers involved in the past year: _____
Estimated number of volunteer hours donated in the past year: _____
Estimated dollar value of volunteer time donated: $_____

FINANCES: Fiscal Health Information

This detailed information is intended to provide the Foundation's board & staff with an important overview of your organization's health. It is __required__ that we have a response to each item listed below.

Current overall operating budget: $_____

Current source of funds (in %):
Federal _____%   Corporate _____% Annual giving _____%   Fees _____%
State ____%   Foundation _____% Endowment income ____%   Contracts ____%
Local ____% Special events _____% Investment Income ____%   Other _____%
(NOTE: Total can be greater than 100% since some categories may overlap)
[Specify]

From your most recent financial audit or Form 990 for year ending ____/____/____ :

Percentage of operating expenses spent on:
    Direct services ____ %   Fundraising ____%   Management ____%

Current Assets_____	Current Liabilities_____
Net Prop/Equip_____	Long-Term Debt_____
LT Investments_____	Total Liabilities_____
Total Assets_____	Total Net Assets_____
Unrestricted Net Assets_____	

Amount of operating reserve funds available: $_____

How many months of operating expenses would this cover? _____

Do you have a _permanently_ restricted Endowment Fund? _____yes ____no
    If "yes", current fund balance $_____

Amount/percentage of operating budget ending in surplus/deficit: (please check)

☐ Surplus $_____ _____% ☐ Deficit $_____ _____%

If there is a deficit, is this a recurring deficit in the past three years?

YES ___ NO ___

Explain reason for deficit

_____
_____
_____
_____

Do you have any current organization loans greater than $50,000?
YES_____ NO_____
If yes, please briefly explain:

_____
_____

LEGAL: Litigation Information

Does your organization have any open matters of litigation currently pending?
YES ____ NO____
If yes, please explain in an attachment to your proposal.

Does your organization carry Directors & Officers Insurance? YES_____ NO_____

RATIOS FOR EVALUATING A NONPROFIT'S FISCAL HEALTH

We have found the following ratios to be helpful in analyzing a nonprofit organization's fiscal health and stability. When completing an analysis, if a ratio is significantly different than the benchmark, it is important to discuss this with the nonprofit. There often are good reasons for why a particular ratio is out of range and, therefore, not a cause for concern.

Topic	Purpose	Benchmark
Current Ratio: assets ÷ liabilities	Measures liquidity – ability to meet current obligations	Greater than or equal to 1
Long-Term Investments: Investments ÷ total assets	Measures long-term liquidity & financial stability	Greater than or equal to 25%
Plant, Property, Equipment: Fixed assets ÷ total assets	Measures liquidity & long-term financial flexibility	Less than or equal to 50%
Long-Term Debt: long-term Debt ÷ total net assets	Measures long-term financial obligations	Less than or equal to 50%
Net Asset Growth: current total net assets minus prior total net assets ÷ prior total net assets	Measures surplus or deficit; surplus shows growth; deficit may indicate a financial red flag	Greater than or equal to the annual CPI
Source Dependence: Largest single revenue source ÷ total revenues	Measures reliance on the single largest revenue source to determine possible lack of fiscal diversity and potential for fiscal vulnerability	Less than or equal to 65% of revenues

Contributions: contributions and grants ÷ revenues	Measures reliance on charitable giving, which can be volatile	Less than or equal to 50%
Programs: program expenses ÷ total expenses	Measures resources spent on programs	Greater than or equal to 70%
Administration: administration expenses ÷ total expenses	Measures resources spent on administration	Less than or equal to 25%
Compensation: salaries, benefits, & taxes ÷ total expenses	Measures resources spent on staff costs	Less than or equal to 70%
Net margin: net surplus ÷ total revenue	Measures % of revenue resulting in surplus or deficit	Greater than or equal to CPI
Grant request proportion: grant request ÷ total expenses	Measures request as a % of total expenses	Less than or equal to 25%

PROPOSAL RATING FORM

Please evaluate the proposal on the degree to which it meets criteria according to this scale:

1 = Not at all   2 = Minimally   3 = Moderately
4 = Substantially   5 = To a High Degree

EVALUATION CRITERIA

Score 1-5:

_____ To what extent does the proposal match (funder's) mission and values?

_____ Does the proposal demonstrate a strong degree of partnering and collaboration?

_____ How well documented is the need for the proposed project?

_____ To what extent does the project demonstrate well-researched and/or time-tested strategies and actions that will help meet the overall project goals?

_____ Are projected outcomes clearly stated and is there a viable plan for measuring them?

_____ Does the organization demonstrate the capacity to conduct the proposed project successfully?

_____ To what degree does this project seem cost effective?

_____ Will the (funder's) funding make a significant difference at this time?

Please indicate strengths and weaknesses of this proposal:

_____

_____

_____

_____

_____

_____

_____

_____

_____

Please give your overall rating of this proposal: _____

Do not Recommend ←-------------------------------→ **Strongly Recommend**

1   2   3   4   5

GRANT AGREEMENT

PLEASE READ CAREFULLY

Upon application of _____ ("Grantee") to the _____ (hereinafter "Grantor"), Grantor agrees to make the following grant award and Grantee agrees to accept such grant, in accordance with the terms below and subject to the additional conditions set forth in the Special Conditions section of this agreement.

DESCRIPTION OF GRANT

GRANTEE:

AMOUNT OF GRANT:

REPORTING SCHEDULE: Interim Report Due:
                                    Final Report Due:

DATE AUTHORIZED:

DURATION OF GRANT:

PAYMENTS SCHEDULE:

SPECIFIC PURPOSES OF THE GRANT: Support for the

_____

Use of Granted Funds. Grant funds and the income therefrom will be used exclusively for charitable, scientific, literary, or educational purposes and specifically for the exclusive benefits of (list any specific populations or areas). Grantee will not use the funds:

> ➤ to carry on propaganda, or otherwise attempt to influence legislation,

- to influence the outcome of any specific public election, or to carry on, directly or indirectly, any voter registration drive,
- to make any grant to an individual for travel, study or other similar purposes by such individual, unless specific requirements are satisfied,
- to make any grant to an organization unless: (1) such organization (a) is a public charity under IRS Code Sections 509(a)(1) or (2); (b) is a Type I, Type II or a functionally integrated Type III supporting organization under Section 509(a)(3) (unless a disqualified person of the Grantee directly or indirectly controls such Type I, Type II or functionally integrated Type III supporting organization or a supported organization of the supporting organization); or (c) is an exempt operating foundation; or (2) the Grantee exercises expenditure responsibility with respect to such grant, or
- to undertake any activity for any purpose that is not a charitable purpose as defined in IRS Code Section 170(c)(2)(B).

Program Monitoring and Evaluation. The Grantor may, at its expense, monitor and conduct an evaluation of operations under this grant, which may include visits by representatives of the Grantor to observe the Grantee's program procedures and operations and to discuss the program with the Grantee's personnel.

Accounting and Financial Review. A complete and accurate record of the funds received and expenses incurred under this grant must be maintained by the Grantee. The Grantor may, at its own expense and on reasonable notice to the Grantee, audit or have audited the records of the grantee insofar as they relate to the activities funded by this grant.

Budget. No changes may be made in the funded project's budgetary allocations without the Grantor's prior written approval.

Continuing Support. By making this grant, the Grantor assumes no obligation to provide future or continuing support for the Grantee. Additionally, during the period in which the Grantee may be receiving multi-year payments on a previously awarded grant, the Grantee agrees not to submit a new grant request until the multi-year payment is completed. Furthermore, if the Grantor's financial status changes negatively, the Grantor reserves the right to cancel future grant payouts on any multi-year commitments it has made.

Reporting. In accordance with the schedule above, the Grantee shall furnish to the Grantor a detailed six-month interim progress report and a written twelve-month final report on: (a) the use of the grant funds as well as an accounting of all expenditures made (including, without limitation, salaries, travel, and supplies); (b) compliance with the terms of the grant; and (c) the progress made by the Grantee toward achieving the purposes for which the grant was made. The content for these reports should be according to the format contained in the "Guidelines for Preparing Progress Reports" provided by the Grantor. Additionally, the Grantor reserves the right not to award any further grants to the Grantee until all reporting requirements for all previous grant awards have been satisfied.

Change in Tax-Exemption Status. Should the Grantee receive notice of a change in its tax-exempt or public charity status from the Internal Revenue Service (e.g., loss of Section 501(c)(3) exemption, becoming a private foundation under Section 509(a), etc.), or if the purpose and mission of the Grantee organization substantially changes, the Grantee must notify the Grantor within ten (10) calendar days of its change in status and/or classification. In the event the grantee's tax-exempt status is revoked, expenditures of grant funds must cease immediately and all unspent funds must be returned to the Grantor.

Publicity. If the grantee wishes to issue a news release concerning the grant, a copy of the proposed release should be submitted to the Grantor for review and approval prior to publication.

Unused Funds. If any or all of the grant is not expended within the duration of the grant period, any funds remaining at the end of the grant period may be applied to the Grantee's general operation. As a matter of good stewardship, however, the Grantee shall inform the Grantor in writing of the intention to do this and state why the grant funds were not able to be spent for the original granted purpose. If approved, Grantor shall inform the Grantee in writing.

Reversion of Grant. All or any portion of the amount granted shall be returned to the Grantor under the following circumstances:

> ➢ If the Grantee loses tax-exempt status under Federal tax laws or substantially changes its purpose and mission,

> ➢ If the Grantee organization ceases to exist or if the Grantee discontinues the project for which the grant is designed before any or all of the grant is expended,

> ➢ If the Grantee fails to comply with any portion of the conditions agreed upon, or

> ➢ If the Grantee uses any portion of the amount granted for purposes other than the specific purposes outlined on the first page of this Grant Agreement.

Record Keeping. Grantee agrees that financial and program records and supporting documentation, including records of receipts and expenditures as well as copies of the reports submitted to the Grantor, will be made available to the Grantor at the conclusion of this grant and, for audit purposes, at the request and expense of the Grantor, for a period of five (5) years from the close of the grant period.

Earnings from Invested Grant Funds. Any earnings which accrue to the Grantee as a result of investing funds awarded under this grant shall be used for the specific purposes of the grant and shall be reported in the financial section of the progress reports submitted to the Grantor.

No Other Conditions. The grant shall not be earmarked for any purpose that would cause the grant to be deemed a "taxable expenditure" within the meaning of Section 4945(d) of the Internal Revenue Code and the Treasury regulations thereunder. As of the date of this Agreement, there does not exist any agreement between the Grantor and the Grantee, oral or written, that the grant shall be earmarked for the use of any secondary grantee, or that that Grantor may cause the selection of a secondary grantee to whom the Grantee may devote all or part of the income from the grant.

Special Conditions. The Grantee accepts and agrees to comply with the following Special Conditions specified by the Grantor:

_____

_____

Intended to be legally bound the Grantor and Grantee have hereafter on this date set forth their hand and seal as follows:

GRANTOR: GRANTEE:

NAME: NAME:
TITLE: TITLE:
DATE: _____   DATE: _____

ADDRESS: ADDRESS:

SIGNED: SIGNED:

_____   _____

GRANT PROGRESS REPORT FORM

For Interim Reports: Please provide as much information as is appropriate.

For Final Reports: Please provide information covering the full grant period.

Grant Award Date from Grant Agreement

_____

Organization Name

_____

Completed by

_____

Date submitted

_____

Interim Report   Due Date _____

Final Report   Due Date _____

___General Operations   ___Program

___Capacity/Technical Assistance   ___Capital

___ Endowment   ___Other _____

ADMINISTRATIVE

Describe any organizational changes, achievements, and/or setbacks that have occurred during the grant period. (Example, board, staff, governance).

Did you receive an Informational Memo with this current grant agreement? ___yes ___ no

If yes, what actions have been taken regarding the items noted in the memo?

EVALUATION

List the original goals and objectives of the grant.

In what ways, if any, did the actual grant-funded activity vary from the initial project plans?

Describe any anticipated/unanticipated outcomes, benefits, or challenges encountered with this project. Describe both quantitative and qualitative outcomes.

To date, what are the most important results and lessons learned from this grant?

How will you utilize what has been learned?

FINANCIAL

What is the strategy for obtaining ongoing general operating support or project funding?

FINANCIAL REPORTING – submit only with the final report

➤ Provide actual income and expenses for the year in which the grant was used.

➤ Using the original budget included in the proposal, provide an itemized budget of actual expenses and income for the project/general operations for the grant period. Provide a brief narrative for variances of 10% or more.

➤ Include a detailed, complete accounting of how the grant dollars were spent.

➤ Who else funded this project, and at what levels?

Name of Executive Director

_____

Signature _____ Date _____

INFORMATIONAL MEMO

This memo is sent to grantees which, as a result of the Governance and Financial assessments conducted during the grant review process, are not meeting the expected benchmarks. The memo can also be useful during the review of any future proposals from the grantee, enabling the reviewer to determine if progress has been made in addressing the deficiencies.

To:

From:

Date:

The Foundation is happy to make a grant this time in response to your recent request for funding support. In reviewing your grant application, however, we have come upon areas you should address as a matter of Best Practice before your next grant request to us. Attention to these items will make your organization a stronger and more fundable one. Please note the following:

(Insert the items here).

Addressing these areas, we believe, will strengthen your position in making the case that you are a strong nonprofit organization worthy of support from the Foundation or other funding agencies you may choose to approach. Please address the progress in these areas when you submit your interim report to us.

If you have any questions, please feel free to give the Foundation a call at

———